Traditional Chinese Plays

Volume 3

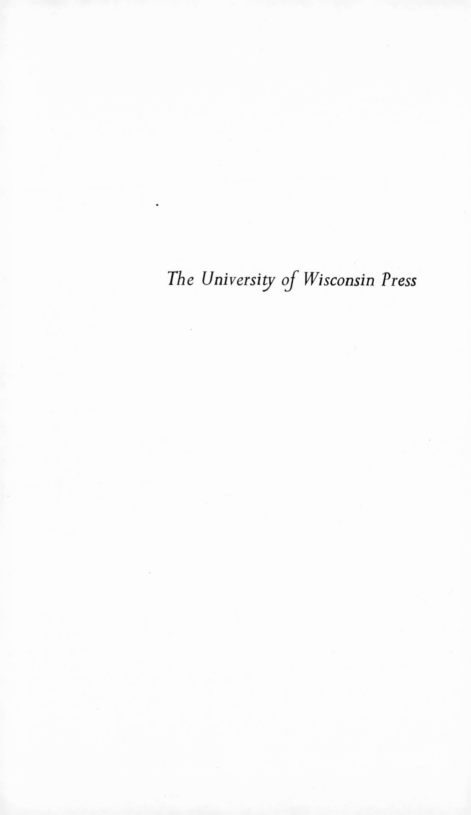

The University of Wisconsin Press

Traditional Chinese Plays

Volume 3
Translated, described, annotated
and illustrated by A. C. Scott

Picking
Up
the Jade
Bracelet
———
Shih
yü-cho

A Girl
Setting
Out
for Trial
———
Nü
ch'i-chieh

Published 1975
The University of Wisconsin Press
Box 1379, Madison, Wisconsin 53701

The University of Wisconsin Press, Ltd.
70 Great Russell Street, London

First printing

Printed in the United States of America

For LC CIP information see the colophon
ISBN 0-299-06630-4

Preface

The aim of this book is to increase understanding of traditional Chinese
stage practice in much the same way as in the two previous volumes. It
differs slightly from them in that it is concerned with the acting style of
one kind of role only, that of the stage clown, or *ch'ou*. To write about
comic acting is "to climb trees for fish" as the Chinese themselves might
say, for the art of the clown depends on the sheer sparkle of his presence
as much as on what he says or does. The unspoken implication, the artful glance, above all his instinct for split-second timing, are intangible
elements which vanish even as they are there. The clown's appeal is immediate precisely because it is so fleeting.

The things which made people laugh a generation ago do not necessarily seem funny today. How much more elusive humor becomes, therefore, when it is the product of a culture quite different from our own.
In any country the clown's rapport with his audience is sharpened by
such factors as national attitudes, social customs, and, of course, the
subtleties of colloquial speech. The last alone is sufficient to complicate
all other problems of interpretation.

Nevertheless, once ethnic factors can be placed in their proper relationship, we arrive on familiar ground. For centuries, food, drink,
elimination, and sex have been obsessive topics for the clown protesting
on behalf of the common man. The Peking comic actor has been no
exception to time-worn tradition. If he seems far removed from our
contemporary sophistication perhaps the answer may be that in today's
complex society we do not always recognize the enduring simplicity of
the language of theater.

It was said in the first volume that Peking play scripts are devices to
release the dynamic processes of the actor rather than examples of literature. The point will not require laboring for readers of these pieces

featuring the comic actor. Although the clown's language is used to implement the reality of meaning differently from the formalized and entirely artificial speech patterns of the other roles, the material is bound to seem contrived when separated from the animating force of the comic actor.

There is an old story current in our own theater circles of the young actor who claimed that success as a comic depended on being faithful to nature. "Nature," retorted a seasoned old performer, "nature be damned! You make them laugh!" Which is to say that however colloquially presented there can be no such thing as "natural" acting, and comedy in fact is a very serious stage business. The Chinese comic actor like his Western counterpart has always been regarded as a master of improvisation, an inveterate ad-libber adept at seizing the immediate moment on the wing. A closer acquaintance reveals that spontaneity is usually sustained by timing that leaves nothing to chance and is carefully calculated to anticipate the mood of the audience and ride it to a climax. Among the four main role categories of the old Peking stage, the clown was the only one empowered to speak in down-to-earth language, indulge in topical or personal allusions, and in general identify himself with the crowd out in front. Yet the improvisatory quality of the performance was bound by the predictability of his stage routines. Like the Commedia dell' Arte, the Peking theater gave full license to the comic spirit through specifically prescribed types from whom the audience demanded their favorite bits of business. These were perfected by generations of actors until they permanently labeled each character. Although personality was important with the master Chinese actor playing the clown, it was always the clown he was playing.

The *ch'ou,* or comic actor, was an essential member of every traditional theatrical troupe in China, and a majority of the plays in the repertoire were designed to provide scope for his entry at some point. As on the Shakespearian stage, an alchemic fusion of the comic with the serious constituted the stock in trade of the Peking theater and gave the repertoire a characteristic flavor. Moreover, just as Shakespeare's audiences represented a cohesive cross-section of a community who were seasoned playgoers as a matter of course, so too the theater in China provided a public focus. A sense of solidarity was induced through dramatic expression of traditional values whose vulnerable points were nonetheless recognized targets for the clown in rousing the laughter of the crowd. The new society which has been fashioned in China has been nurtured on the principle that destructive laughter is socially detrimental to the class struggle in the theater as elsewhere; the Peking repertoire has been superseded by a category of plays in which, significantly, there are no clowns.

In former times the recognized levels of Chinese society were defined by the Four Classes (*ssu-min*), scholar, farmer, artisan, and merchant. Ample scope was provided there for fertile variations on the theme of the "establishment" against "us," and theater throve on this fact. China's patriarchal family system and elite literary minority in control of a peasant majority offered the classic situation for the clown's talents. In China as elsewhere he was always ready to turn to that old standby of popular entertainment, the confrontation of the ordinary man with the learned. That is not to ignore the fact that the comic actor drew upon the characteristics of a variety of human types for the pleasure of his audiences, but the innate shrewdness of the peasant, his transparent simplicity of outlook and unabashed recognition of physical needs were beyond all else the qualities shared with the clown. His role called for the same quintessence of unregenerate human nature to inspire his perfect communion with the crowd.

The two pieces translated in this book were perennial favorites with the audiences of Peking, Shanghai, and Nanking, and it was a rare occasion indeed when one or another of them was not being staged somewhere in the theater quarters of those cities. Each of these pieces is in fact a complete scene extracted from a much longer play. Both of them have stood the test of time as independent entertainment in their own right simply because they offered ideal material for the master actor to display his virtuosity according to the canons. Although in both plays the heroine provides a focus of attention, the one for her coquettish mime and the other for the graceful quality of her sung narrative, no Chinese audience could have imagined them complete without the artful presence of the clown. He by the very nature of his role is customarily confined to a supporting function, but this in itself lends added piquancy to those moments when he takes over the whole stage, as he frequently does in these two pieces, keeping the pace going with an élan that eludes capture by any written description.

On this note it may be timely to restate the intention behind this series of translations, which is, first, to offer theater students an acceptable compromise for understanding the methods of a vanishing dramatic genre and, second, to provide a descriptive record of the old Peking theater world for less specialized readers. A distinction is implicit in the word compromise, for it must be said again that these translations are not meant as complete production scripts for Western directors. They can, it is hoped, be useful guides for workshop production, given the presence of a trained Chinese performer and the availability of authentic music on tapes. The two usually go together these days and are not impossible to find, in the United States at least, although admittedly they do not grow on every tree. These texts, therefore, in so far as they can serve any production purposes, are based on the assumption that the obvious motive for Western theater students exploring the technicalities of Asian acting forms lies in their being able to work at close quarters with a trained Asian specialist. They may then become intensely conscious of space, movement, control, economy of expression, and the true meaning of style in a way that is impossible by any other means. In the need to achieve precise and harmonious control of their physical energy as revealed in the seemingly effortless skill of the Asian instructor, students are induced to confront their own clichés and evasions, to shed their self-esteem to a point where they ask themselves why they are on the stage at all. Showmanship and spectacle, the seducers of so many Western enthusiasts for Eastern theater, do not help the theater student forced to confront the stark essentials of theatrical discipline with nothing but his own physical inadequacy, an empty stage, and the keen eye of the Asian artist/teacher as witness to the challenge.

These principles have been a force behind our Asian theater studies in the University of Wisconsin and have influenced the preparation of these scripts as accessories to empirical studies. Authentic Chinese theater, or indeed any form of Asian theater, cannot be transplanted by the means of translations which in themselves must always be one remove from authenticity. To repeat what has been said, they are a compromise. A text translated as a key to what happens on the stage rather than as a literary study is likely to serve a more enlightening purpose for the theater student. One reviewer used the term "blueprint" to describe a previous volume, and this may be an acceptable definition provided it is understood that blueprints are best interpreted in practice by those with the necessary technical training.

In contrast to our own play scripts, which provide a director with the necessary and often detailed information for the disposition of his actors and the interpretation of time, place, and mood, a Chinese play text offers virtually nothing at all. The most cursory instructions suffice. "On," "off," "speaks," "laughs," "sings in so and so rhythm" comprise a major vocabulary of stage directions. A script merely states the stark points of progression for an interpretation by an actor who has mastered his form to the point where it is instinctive and instantaneously called into being. The major concern of the Chinese actor was to come to terms with the spatial area he had to control, whether it was a bare stage twenty feet square or an equally bare stage twice those dimensions. He had no more need of a script than his audience, for whom the actor was the play.

The Chinese texts used for these translations were part of a series called The Revised Peking Play Series, *Kai-liang ching-hsi pen,* published by Ch'en Ts'u-ming of the Shanghai Drama Study Association, *Shanghai hsi-hsüeh shu chü,* at the Chia-t'ing Book Company, *Chia-t'ing shu-sha, Honan-lu,* Shanghai. None of the texts are dated, but the series was probably published some forty years ago. *Picking Up the Jade Bracelet* was translated from the complete text of *At the Temple of Buddhist Doctrine, Ch'üan-pu Fa-men ssu,* edited by Chao Jui-t'ang. *A Girl Setting Out for Trial* was translated from the complete text of *Jade Pavilion of Happiness, Ch'üan-pu Yü-t'ang ch'un,* edited by Lin Ju-nung and Ch'en Hsi-hsin.

Acknowledgments

I must acknowledge my debt to Wang Te-k'un, a young *ch'ou* actor who gave so freely of his knowledge and experience for my benefit in the past. Although our association was cut short by the political events of twenty-five years ago the memory of his stage presence remains. I want to thank Miss Hu Hung-yen, now of New York, a *hua-tan* actress who has been of such great assistance to me in my work over a long period of time, both in the United States and Hongkong. I would like to acknowledge my former language teacher, Mrs. Shu-hsiu Macdonald, now of the University of Leeds, England, who helped me in so many ways during my early study of the theater in Nanking. I also want to thank Professor Liu Wu-chi of Indiana University for his expert reading of my manuscript and his advice on my translation. A final tribute is due to my students past and present at the University of Wisconsin. I shall not forget their enthusiasm, dedication, and affection.

A. C. S.

University of Wisconsin
1974

Contents

Illustrations

LINE DRAWINGS *by the author*   *Page*

Introduction

Introduction

The Role of the Comic Actor in the Peking Theater

Chinese theater people always list the comic role last in order of the four principal categories which defined the Peking actor's techniques, i.e. *sheng,* male; *tan,* female; *ching,* painted face; and *ch'ou,* comic. There is a rather complicated history behind these names because the Chinese propensity for classification led to the use of a multiplicity of subtitles, the better to identify several variations of the main acting styles. As new acting forms were devised many of the role designations acquired new implications. During the last one hundred and fifty years, a period when the Peking theater reached its zenith, there were many new developments in acting and in consequence the creation of new definitions. Some of these superseded the old names, others became alternatives, many of them have continued in use until today, although not always with complete consistency, by the Chinese themselves.

Ch'i Ju-shan,[1] a most erudite historian of the traditional Peking

1. Ch'i Ju-shan (1876-1962) was a classically educated Chinese scholar who visited Europe in his youth after studying French and German. In 1914 he became associated with the actor Mei Lan-fang, then embarking on an illustrious career, resulting in an artistic partnership which endured for more than twenty years. Ch'i wrote more than twenty plays for Mei, many of them based on his researches into the ancient dance and he remained a constant adviser to the actor in all matters concerning his stage art. When Mei toured America in 1930 he was accompanied by Ch'i. Their partnership ended in 1931 after the Japanese attack on Manchuria, and Mei moved from Peking to Shanghai. During the thirties Ch'i published a series of books embodying the results of his theatrical research and he also founded a museum and research center. Ch'i had an encyclopedic knowledge of theater matters and was the first Chinese scholar to concern himself with live theater rather than literary theory, and with the problems of the actor. He spent a

3

theater, considered that the *ch'ou* role used not to be a separate category at all but simply a version of the *ching,* or painted face role, which itself underwent a whole new stage of development during the nineteenth century. Eventually attempts to distinguish the particular characteristics of the comic actor resulted in the use of the terms *hsiao hua-lien,* "small painted face" and *san hua-lien,* "tri-painted face," presumably derived from the clown's make-up style. The first of these two terms is now used by theater people to identify talkative, wisecracking characters such as servants, small tradesmen, rustics, and the like, while the second term has become yet one more generic description for the comic role.

Not content with this degree of differentiation, the Chinese also liked to classify their favourite comic roles as being either *wen* or *wu,* names which were used to categorize the music and plays of the Peking stage as well as the actors' roles. *Wen* implies theater dealing with everyday life and people; whether the setting is a cottage or a mansion is beside the point. By far the greater number of comic parts were *wen* roles, including the *hsiao hua-lien* mentioned above. *Wu* on the other hand indicates a style of performance requiring vigorous and often violent action such as fighting, acrobatics, sword displays, and so on. The *wu-ch'ou* actor was a comparative newcomer to the traditional Peking stage, having been introduced during the last hundred years or so as new plays requiring this type of role were devised for the repertoire. Great skill was demanded from the *wu-ch'ou* performer whom theatergoers also labeled with the picturesque title of *k'ai k'ou t'iao,* or "open the mouth and jump" actor.

There was seemingly no end to the Chinese fondness for labels in their theater. The *wen-ch'ou* classification was sometimes broken down into *ta ch'ou,* "big comic," role and *hsiao ch'ou,* "small comic," role, the latter being the same as the "small painted face" genre already named. The "big comic" role usually meant a part in which the actor wore the *mang,* a robe only used by officials in the old days. Government by a tightly centralized system of scholar bureaucrats, who for centuries remained the backbone of China's famed civil service, offered

---

large part of his time in the theater and was at his best surrounded by theater people. It was in his lively conversation that his immense depth of theatrical knowledge was revealed. Ch'i, who spent the last decade of his life in Taiwan, was a unique force in the revival of the traditional Chinese theater during the twenties and thirties and until the end of his days remained its most cogent spokesman.

Drawing 1. Actor in the role of a comic scholar during the early years
of this century.

obvious material for the comic actor, the more so as the rise of the popular Peking theater corresponded with a decline in the quality and integrity of government. Corruptness and stupidity at all levels provided the basis for many well known interpretations of officialdom on the stage.

There remains a third major category of the comic role to be considered, *ch'ou-p'o*. The word *p'o* means a woman getting on in years, a mother-in-law, a stepmother, at any rate a shrewish female, typical of whom is Liu the marriage go-between[2] in *Picking Up the Jade Bracelet*.

2. The professional marriage go-between, or matchmaker (*mei-p'o*) was an indispensable figure in traditional Chinese society and a legacy from the ancient patrilineal clan laws which decreed that marriage was a matter for family decision and not an individual choice. Under the patriarchal system authority was exercised exclusively by the father and, failing him, the eldest son of the family, assisted by the "unctuous word of the go-between" when a betrothal was to be arranged.

Ancient marriage ritual rested on what were called the "six rites" and these influenced family conduct until very recent times. They consisted of (1) sending gifts by messenger to ascertain whether a particular girl was marriageable or not, (2) enquiring into the particulars of a girl's birth, (3) deciding whether the marriage would be both appropriate and auspicious, (4) paying a marriage settlement, (5) requesting a date to be fixed for the wedding, (6) welcoming the bride home by the bridegroom. A go-between was responsible for initiating these proceedings and attending to their details.

Once a girl reached marriageable age the go-between was called in. It was understood that a prospective married couple should have the same social background and means, and the go-between began by writing down the birth date of the girl, the year, month, day and hour, on a slip of paper called the "eight character" paper. In Chinese thinking, the universe was composed of Heaven and Earth elements to each of which were attributed a specific number of causative influences. A harmonious combination of these dependent on the birth signs of the couple concerned was the prerequisite for a successful marriage. At this point the diviner or fortuneteller was usually called in to assist the go-between. The details on the eight character slip were far more important than good looks in the selection of a bride, and until the diviner declared the omens favorable, a go-between was obliged to run constantly to and fro between the parties. Once these matters were satisfactorily smoothed out the go-between had the task of arranging the terms of the marriage settlement between the two families and deciding on a suitable date for a formal betrothal ceremony, this being marked by a reciprocal exchange of gifts between the two families. The young couple's fate was then sealed.

Professional marriage go-betweens were usually women although men were not unknown in this capacity. In more recent times friends or acquaintances of a family have performed the function on an amateur basis, the important thing being a sufficient knowledge of both families to bring about successful negotiations.

Diplomacy, a shrewd sense of bargaining, and a touch of the old rogue suggest the necessary qualities of the old time professional marriage go-between who, at a

The shrew was a familiar figure in the old Chinese family system where a mother-in-law could be a tyrant to strike dread into the heart of many a young bride, while the professional matchmaker not infrequently earned the reputation of being a devious schemer trading in human relationships. Chinese audiences were always tickled by the sight of the stage clown parodying these formidable women with a cunning attention to detail. Among all the roles played by the comic actor none was more wickedly mischievous in its reality of characterization than that of the shrewish female.

In some ways this character was reminiscent of the old English music-hall "dame," that dominating and frequently bibulous gossip who was a favorite of London audiences in the early years of the century. Her proletarian style was also the creation of male ingenuity. The Chinese equivalent, it is true, was unconcerned with alcholic indulgence in the way of the music-hall droll, but only because drinking in China was a very different kind of social custom outside the experience of ordinary women, who had no peers, however, as gossips and domestic tyrants!

That is not to say that the Chinese clown has lagged behind in portraying intoxication, a subject dear to the comic actor down the ages. A notable example is the play *The Drunken Yamen Runner* from the repertoire of the regional K'unshan theater. It seems only natural that the earthy inventiveness of the Chinese comic owed much to theatrical forms which were the direct expression of local communities. China abounds with regional dramatic styles in whose development and cross development the long and complex history of her theater must be sought. Such regional styles, particularly those of central and eastern China, contributed a great deal to the growth of a comic acting tradition on the Peking stage, where it was perfected by talented nineteenth-century actors who were well versed in the K'unshan style. This regional form, it will be recalled, attained a national prominence and influenced the acting styles of the Peking theater in several ways during a formative period.

The Drunken Yamen Runner was developed from an incident in a longer play and survived on its own merits long after the original had disappeared from the stage. The plot of the play concerned a young

---

lower level, was often credited with the shadier practice of procurement. One attitude towards the class was summed up by an old saw which ran: "A matchmaker does not have to live a lifetime with the people he brings together," a sardonic comment on a social institution which was given scant mercy on the stage.

gentleman-scholar, a type of hero found in scores of stage love stories, who became infatuated with a celebrated sing-song girl but failed in his attempts to meet her personally. His friend, in the person of the District Magistrate,[3] came to the rescue by smuggling the girl into the *yamen*,[4] disguising her in clothing proper to a respectable maiden and arranging a meeting in the flower garden. It was a case of love at first sight, and unknown to the magistrate the pair arranged to meet at the young scholar's house next day, which happened to be that most romantic of all Chinese holidays, the Moon Festival.[5] It was from here that *The*

3. The District Magistrate, or *chih-hsien,* was the man at the bottom of the ladder of high officialdom and the cog which kept the wheels of local government turning. He was responsible for order in his territory, the administration of justice and the collection of taxes among several other functions. The Chinese often referred to him as the "father-mother official," *fu-mu kuan.* Serving under him was a small hierarchy of assistants and petty officials, as well as private secretaries and servants who were his personal employees. The District Magistrate was directly responsible to the Provincial authorities and through them to supreme authority in the national capital. Although he was empowered to recommend the death sentence for crimes, this always had to be reviewed and the case retried by his Provincial superiors who in turn were subject to the final decision of the Board of Punishment in the Imperial capital. The nature of his position understandably laid the District Magistrate open to all kinds of pressures and to bribery. Popular opinion of officialdom during the last years of Imperial China is summed up in the cynical remarks of the old warder in the play *A Girl Setting Out For Trial,* representing a point of view which is echoed in a number of plays. In fairness it must be added that the just and honest official was equally given his due in the traditional Chinese theater.

4. The *yamen* was at once the private residence and official quarters of any official who held the government's seal of authority under the old Imperial civil service in China. In this case it refers to the premises occupied by the District Magistrate and his entourage and families. There was a proverb, "The fourth assistant magistrate has two more teeth than the second," *ssu-ya pi erh-ya to liang-ya,* a reference to the corruptness of officialdom and an example of the Chinese fondness for word play both on and off the stage. The word *ya* meaning tooth has the same sound as the word *ya* in *yamen* although the written characters are different. Official cupidity was the mainstay of many a theatrical plot on the old stage.

5. The Moon Festival (*yüeh-hsi*), or Mid-Autumn Festival (*chung-ch'iu*), according to the Chinese lunar calendar was celebrated on the fifteenth day of the eighth month, i.e., towards the end of our September. On that day the moon is at its brightest and fullest, and it was the custom when dusk fell to hold wine-drinking parties out of doors to admire the beauty of the moonlight. Special cakes filled with fruit and spices were made and placed on the family altars and offered to neighbors as gifts. The custom of making "moon cakes" still persists although the

Drunken Yamen Runner[6] took up the tale. Innocent of the intrigue, the magistrate ordered his official runner to go to the young scholar's address with an invitation to a moon-viewing party. The runner, already hazy in mind and unsteady of step through his own celebrations, was nevertheless compelled to obey orders. The play depicts his unwilling and erratic progress interlarded with vinous comments on the character of officialdom. The comical climax comes when he arrives at his destination where the young scholar sunk in romantic reverie awaits the arrival of his love. He is unexpectedly roused by the runner who with tipsy humour simulates the voice of a girl, a favorite bit of business with Chinese clowns and storytellers.

The Drunken Yamen Runner[7] was divided into two scenes, the first being devoid of any stage properties while in the second a small wooden table and chair, both covered with embroidered silk hangings, were placed rear center stage. Behind the table sat the young scholar, right elbow squarely planted on the table and tilted head supported on the right hand which was concealed by the ample white silk "water sleeve," a traditional posture for a sleeping character, marking the scene as set for the final hilarious confrontation. This little mime piece provided great scope for the comic actor. His manipulation of spatial area with nothing more than pantomime and gesture, precisely timed by the beat of drum and gong, evoked the catalytic genius of the stage clown's talent in its most primal sense.

The comic actors of the Peking theater brought to life a colorful

-----

commercial products produced by modern bakeries tend to be somewhat more indigestible than the old homemade products!

As this festival seems to have connections with fertility ritual, it has always been regarded as one special to women and autumn as a time propitious for marriage. The Moon Festival, therefore, used to be an occasion when girls traditionally offered up their silent prayers for a suitable husband.

6. *Yamen* runner: There were a number of petty functionaries attached to every District Magistrate's headquarters including the runners, *ya-i,* who acted as messengers, guards, and policemen. They were organized under four categories, one of which was the *tsao-li,* or lictor, and it is to this category that the runner in this play belongs. *Tsao* means black and *li* is a generic term for an underling. The name is derived from the black uniform which these men wore.

7. *The Drunken Yamen Runner, Tsui-tsao,* was based on an incident from the play called *Red Pear Chronicle, Hung-li chi,* contained in an anthology of plays popular in the Yüan, Ming, and Ch'ing dynasties and first published in the eighteenth century under the title *A Coat of Fine Furs, Chui pai-ch'iu.* It was published in a four volume edition in Peking in 1955.

gallery of characters on stage. The list is interminable, including as it does peasants, crafty servants, court intriguers, pedantic bureaucrats, and downright rogues in all their manifestations, with vices ranging from gambling and lechery to plain murder. The Chinese have always been interested in man the fallible rather than in his spiritual aspirations, and in the clown's portrayals their interest was indulged to the full.

The dwarf and the hunchback, figures familiar to us from the history of the court fools in Europe, were likewise to be found in the Peking clown's repertoire. There they were stock figures simulated by skillful mimetic techniques and grotesque make-up which in themselves provided stock usage. A play which used to bring the house down in Peking in the old days was one featuring two characters who were a byword among the Chinese themselves, the dwarf Wu Ta-lang and his wife P'an Chin-lien, a lady of easy virtue. The name of the dwarf passed into usage as being synonymous for the personification of the "little man." Even a tiger would not eat him, it was said, for he did not appear to be a man at all.

Five Flower Grotto, Wu Hua Tung, the play in question, portrays the impersonation of the dwarf and his wife by two temple spirits, resulting in a hilarious scene between the true and the false couples. This is further complicated when the real dwarf lays a complaint before the magistrate, who turns out to be a dwarf himself. At one time this play was turned into an extravaganza in which the dwarf and his wife were impersonated in quintuple. The effect of five dwarfs and five wives on the stage simultaneously can be imagined.

Playing a dwarf calls for considerable physical stamina on the part of the comic actor, who must move around the stage the whole time in a crouching posture, literally sitting on his haunches and moving along with a rapid heel and toe movement of the feet to propel himself forward. It naturally puts great strain on the legs and waist, and the technique was only acquired in the arduous years of apprentice training.

In the play mentioned, the dwarf Wu Ta-lang was portrayed wearing a drooping mustache and the traditional patch of white make-up round the nose and eyes. His cap was of dark blue wool with a fringed crown, usually worn by characters of humble status and menial occupation on the Chinese stage, and he had a lighter blue cotton robe with a crossover neck line. A white silk skirt was secured round his waist completely hiding his legs. Both robe and skirt were cut proportionately to his reduced stature and to accent the illusion of his deformity.

An example of a hunchback played by the comic actor may be cited

Drawing 2. Hu-lun the hunchback

in the play *T'o-tzu chiao ch'in, The Hunchback Snatches a Wife.* The theme tells of Hu-lun, the ugly younger son of a Sung emperor, who fell in love with the daughter of a high official when he passed her in the palace grounds. He sent a matchmaker to press his suit, but the mother of the girl insisted that the preliminary interview between them should take place on the city wall. Hu-lun sent his good-looking elder brother to stand in for him, and the match was successfully negotiated. When the hunchback himself went to claim his bride the horrified parents refused to let their daughter go, and the angry suitor thereupon resorted to kidnaping.

Although the hunchback is still a figure of fun in this play there is a malevolence to him quite different from the character of the previously described dwarf, who is a pure buffoon. As a person of rank, the hunchback wears court dress, and some idea of his appearance may be conveyed by the illustration. Though far from being a Richard III, there was a sense of evil generated in the role of Hu-lun which placed him beyond the borderline of the clown's normal territory.

If, as Dr. Johnson remarked, "comedy has been particularly unpropitious to its definers," at least in the Western world it has been possible to trace historical development of the clown's art with some degree of continuity. The Greek and Roman mimes, the wandering buffoons of the feudal era, the court jesters of the Middle Ages, and the Commedia dell'Arte all have been given their place in the ancestral line of the professional stage clown. They were important elements in a pattern of evolution with ritual origins whose religious and clerical functions became transmuted for secular purposes, finally leading to the relegation of ritualistic solemnity and the emergence of professional comic types.

In Asia and China specifically, the history of the clown remains open to much greater conjecture. The circumstances of Asian cultural assimilation have been so complex and have encompassed such a tremendous time span that knowledge of the theatrical past remains fragmentary. The many similarities between the classical Indian and the ancient Chinese theater, for example, remain largely unresolved and in the case of the stage clown, there are many apparent resemblances to provoke speculation and comparison.[8]

8. The *Natyasastra,* the ancient Hindu text on theater, centuries ago defined general principles which underlie so much Asian dramatic philosophy. In categorizing the nature of character roles, the clown, or *vidusaka,* was described as being a dwarf and a hunchback, and although Sanskrit dramatists did not necessarily follow this instruction to the letter in all their plays, it makes an interesting point of com-

In China certainly it would be possible to cite with justification a long history of court jesters, fairground entertainers, and storytellers as the forerunners of a comic stage tradition. The storyteller especially invites credence as a seminal influence.

The art of the storyteller has always been enormously popular in China as in the rest of Asia and has persisted with an astonishing vigor through the centuries. Essentially an entertainment of the market place, the fairgrounds, the teahouse, and the riverboat, storytelling has been practiced by men whose task it was to keep an audience engrossed and the hat passing round. If they lacked a sense of the dramatic their audience simply vanished like smoke and the storyteller's rice bowl remained empty. Small wonder then that from the storytellers' ranks there evolved a class of exceedingly sharp funny men whom nothing escaped as new material for entertaining their patrons.

In China the craft of storytelling covers a wide variety of genres including ballad singers, narrators performing to string or percussion instruments, as well as mimics relying solely on their verbal cunning and imitative skill. Included among this last group are the immensely popular funny men of Peking who are known as *hsiang-sheng*, which literally translated means "imitating sounds." These performers have a technique which shows noticeable affinities with the methods of the stage clown. According to some Chinese authorities their ancestry can be traced to the court jesters who operated some two thousand years ago and were noted for barbed quips about their superiors.

These Peking funny men work singly or in pairs and use no props or musical accompaniment of any kind. They perform in everyday clothes and always carry a folding fan in their hand. Their repertoire is a brilliant mixture of narration, mimicry, wisecracks, and sheer acting skill coupled with a biting wit and superb powers of observation. A speciality of these performers was the impersonation of well known traditional theater stars' mannerisms and their technical interpretations of favorite plays. After skillfully enacting some particular scene dear to the hearts of the fans in this way, the two comics would then bring the house

---

parison with descriptions of the Chinese comic actor. The *Natyasastra* also divided character types into classes, of which there were four for the principal male roles with a corresponding number for the comic roles. The many similarities between ancient Indian and Chinese stage practices suggest something more than coincidence, although the subject has never been explored enough by scholars from either country to substantiate any relationships.

down with some irreverent anticlimax making a nonsense of the whole thing.

A similar approach can be found in *The Butterfly Dream,* translated in the first volume of this series. At the beginning of this play the coquettish heroine performs an airily seductive dance according to the conventions of the role, which is immediately parodied by the clown as soon as she has left the stage. In the play *A Girl Setting Out for Trial,* translated in this volume, the heroine, moved by the self-pity of an old man, offers to become his adopted daughter. Immediately the ritual of filial respect is accomplished, the old man launches into the most irreverent and contemporary references about his new daughter, so reducing stage melodrama to everyday farce. It is in moments like these that the artistic affinity of the stage clown with the *hsiang-sheng* performers is most discernible.

All Chinese traditional acting has its roots in a long tradition whose continuity has been maintained by drawing on many contributory sources, not least among which can be counted the storyteller. The comic actor as he appears in this book, however, could justly be described as an artistic phenomenon of the entertainment world of nineteenth-century Peking. He was the product of a highly professional urban theater, demanding in the standards imposed upon its actors, who daily played to a critical public of devotees.

Some Comments on the Comic Actor's Techniques

The comic actor of the old Peking theater is bound by conventions and strict technical usage, whether it is in speech and song, movement and gesture, or costume and make-up, in the same way as the players in the other three major role categories. It is true, however, that there is a freedom and exaggeration in everything the comic actor says and does and not infrequently an earthiness springing from the very nature of his role, in which a nimble wit, a sense of satire, and a predilection for pure tomfoolery are important qualities for cultivation. Much of the comic actor's technique, therefore, is a more outrageous development of practices observed in the other main roles; much of it is entirely peculiar to himself, not least in the license to improvise and to draw upon sly or suggestive allusions.

VOCAL TECHNIQUES

Dialect has always been a repository of earthy wisdom in any country, and one reason why regional theatrical forms in China contributed so much to the evolution of a vigorous comic acting tradition was undoubtedly their access to rich veins of salty humor. There are eight principal dialects in China, the Northern, Kiangsu-Chekiang, Hunan, Kiangsi, Hakka, Fukien, Southern Fukien, and Kwangtung dialects. By far the most widely spoken is the Northern dialect of which the speech of Peking is a version whose rich burr and rolling *r*'s give such a rumbustious quality to the comic actor's performance. The stage speech of the Peking theater proper contains something from the dialects of Szechuan, Hopei, and Anhui as well as Peking. Its highly formalized structure and strict regard for rhyming systems, as well as the use of romantic metaphor, give added contrast to the brisk colloquial of the comic actor. When he bursts upon the stage it is as though a gust has wafted the sounds of bustling street vendors and shopkeepers right into the theater.

That is not to infer that the comic actor uses colloquial and nothing else; he employs heightened speech some of the time, and it is not without its own formal conventions. It is common to hear the comic actor's voice rising and dying away to a patterned crescendo of sound on the finale of some voluble passage. From time to time he also lapses into short bouts of song. Liu the go-between in *Picking Up the Jade Bracelet* is a good example. Traditional musical metrical patterns are followed, although the colloquial is largely preserved, and the singing in effect becomes a mimicking of the polished artificiality of the true Peking song style, evincing a raucous quality which leaves little doubt about the intent. Sung passages of this kind emphasize a particular confirmation of feelings very often, as, for example, when Liu the go-between sings, "I knew what those two were up to . . . ."

A vocal convention commonly employed by the comic actor is a technique called *shu-pan* "announcing it with the clappers," which is precisely what happens. In this technique the actor suddenly switches from ordinary speech to a rhymed monologue whose timing is beaten out on the wooden clappers manipulated in the left hand of the leader of the orchestra. The effect is gained by selecting words, i.e., Chinese characters, which belong to identical rhyming classes as they are enumerated in the standard formula of rhyming keys for use on the Peking stage. This type of narrative has a continuous, almost breathless quality which is reinforced by the rhythm of the actor's movements and his facial expressions. Frequently this technique is used by the comic actor to make his exit with suitable climatic effect or, facing the audience, to take his opening lines from the center of the stage.

MOVEMENT AND GESTURE

It would be impossible in a short account of this nature to try and go into exhaustive detail about movement and gesture as they relate to the comic actor and his performance, but some general points are worth noting. The entry movement used by all actors when wearing "water sleeves," the long white silk cuffs attached to the orthodox sleeves of a stage costume, is a signal to the rest of the stage, a sign that the actor is about to commence. After taking his stance before the audience, the actor sweeps his right hand, palm inwards, from the chest down to the right knee and then with a turn of the wrist flings the sleeve backwards and upwards to the right. The actor is usually erect with feet firmly placed in position, creating a graceful and often powerful movement. Now with the comic actor it is far less dignified; he stands with his feet well apart and knees bent while the sleeve movement itself is comparatively short and abrupt.

In the male roles the normal walking pace entails placing the feet squarely on the ground six inches or so apart. The right foot is then lifted forward about fourteen inches and the left foot brought up to the right heel and at right angles to it, toes pointing towards the right of course. After a brief pause, the left foot is lifted forward to repeat the movement and in this way the actor moves forward in stately fashion. When the costume of a very high official is worn the steps are much "squarer," that is to say, the feet are moved from side to side. The comic actor uses a little of all of these techniques, but adds his own interpretation. When he is wearing a high official's costume his steps are basically the same as those described but his legs are bent, his body thrust forward a little to swing right and left from the waist. A walk of this kind symbolizes a disreputable character. When he wears informal costume, the comic actor lifts his legs fairly high but his steps are small and there is a movement of the shoulders resulting from the swing of the waist. When wearing the costume used by servants, waiters, and similar characters, the comic actor walks with bent legs lifted fairly high but with rapid steps.

When running, the comic actor uses one of two methods if he is in informal costume. In the first the legs are bent, the head remains fixed but the sleeved arms are waved backwards and forwards against the body. In the second method the body is thrust well forward and very small rapid steps are taken. When wearing the costume of servants and such characters, the comic actor runs quite freely and naturalistically. It should be added that actors of any role seldom run when wearing official costume.

When portraying a dwarf, the comic actor first squats with knees fully bent, body straight, and elbows pressed tightly in to his sides as he poises himself on his toes. He then moves forward so that with each step his body is inclined forwards as the sole of each foot alternately touches his rump before coming down on the heel. His clenched fists move up and down in rhythmical accompaniment to this movement, which, as remarked earlier, can only be attempted by those with years of long training behind them.

When portraying a hunchback, the comic actor uses this gait. One foot is poised on the toe with the knee bent and with the other foot at right angles to it but placed to the rear. The actor limps forward on the poised foot, then brings the other foot up into position again with each step. Padded costume is used to simulate spinal deformities.

When boarding a boat, the actor raises the right knee and hops forward on the right foot, at the same time raising the left foot, the body then swaying gently to and fro to simulate the motion of a boat. When rowing the boat along, the comic actor grasps a wooden oar, with one hand holding the top of the shaft and the other the shaft just above the blade. The oar is held to one side of the body, which is bent forward from the waist. One leg is poised on the toes, knee bent, the other is also bent but with the foot squarely on the ground. From this position the actor moves off, thrusting the oar backwards and forwards with a deliberate emphasis suggesting the resistance of water and alternately moving through the posture described as the actor propels himself forward.

When Chinese troupes toured Australia and New Zealand in 1956, Europe in 1958, and Canada in 1960, audiences were delighted with a short mime-dance-song piece called *Autumn River* adapted for the Peking stage from a regional prototype. This little play concerns a kind-hearted but mischievous old ferryman who is asked to take a pretty girl across the river to enable her to catch up with "someone." The scene where the girl boards the boat is a brilliant example of mime as performed by the comic actor who plays the old ferryman. After much

straining to punt the boat out of the shallows with his charming passenger aboard, the old man "discovers" that they are stuck in the mud.
He takes off his shoes, carefully rolls up his breeches, gingerly tests the
temperature of the water with his wiggling toes, and finally steps into
the shallows where with Herculaean effort he tries to heave the boat off,
standing with his back to the craft and straining with his arms behind
him grasping the sides of the boat. Suddenly his attention becomes
riveted on the bank and roaring with laughter he points out to his, by
now, thoroughly alarmed passenger that he has forgotten to untie the
mooring rope. Splashing ashore, in another graphic interlude he uncoils
the mooring rope, tosses it on the boat, and finally follows with a
tremendous bound that sets his nervous passenger bobbing up and down
like a cork. Needless to say, there is no boat or prop of any kind except
the oar used in this piece, which is remarkable for its pantomimic clarity.

The influence of the *k'un-ch'ü* theater on the Peking style during its
formative years has previously been remarked upon. This influence has
been strong in the case of the comic roles. Many well-known actors who
made their contributions to the Peking-style theater were trained in *k'un-
ch'ü* in their youth, and two in particular, Yang Ming-yü and Liu Kan-
san, were comic actors whose art became legendary and who have left a
stamp on a tradition.[9]

9. According to the few personal facts available, Yang Ming-yü was a native of
Soochow (Su-chou), where he was apprenticed to a training troupe from which he
graduated to a professional company in Tsinan, the capital of Shantung province.
From there he went to Peking, where probably some time during the 1820s he
joined the famous *Ssu-hsi pan,* in which company he began specializing in the
comic roles of the *k'un-ch'ü* repertoire. Regarded as one of the four great Peking
troupes of the period, the *Ssu-hsi pan* specialized in the older repertoire although
it eventually turned to the new Peking-style plays in deference to changing public
tastes. In later years the leader of this troupe was Mei Yü-t'ien, the grandfather of
Mei Lan-fang who has described Yang Ming-yü's technical prowess in his memoirs.

Yang the Third, Yang-san, as he was popularly known, seems to have been
remarkable not only for his comic talents but for the skill and verve of his acrobatics and dancing. One of his famous roles was that of Lou the Rat in the play
Fifteen Strings of Cash, translated in the second volume of this series. According
to those who remember Yang, his technical virtuosity was unsurpassed and no one
on the Peking stage equalled him afterwards, for apparently Yang was such a
martinet as a teacher that few disciples survived his methods, which must have been
fearsome considering the normal rigid standards which prevailed in those days. On
another note, Mei has recorded how in childhood he remembered Yang's skill in
making kites and inventing new styles to try out in the spring winds of Peking.

Yang seems to have ended his days in poverty and obscurity, and his death is

Posture, gesture, and stance, as the Peking actor uses them, in many cases come from *k'un-ch'ü* sources, and the few examples that follow are some common to both styles. Characteristic elements of Chinese acting technique are the pointing gestures which are made using the forefinger as a point of focus, and frequently carried out in time to recitative or music, and extending the sleeve movements. The wagging finger is indispensable to the comic actor in his soliloquies and when scolding his audience.

When he wishes to point behind himself, the comic actor leans forward from the waist with his right foot squarely on the ground, directed obliquely right, while his left leg, bent at the knee, is thrust forward poised on the toes. His right arm is extended in a straight line from the shoulder to his rear while the left arm is bent across the chest, index finger pointing in line with the rear pointing right hand. His head is directed straight ahead at the audience.

When he points to the ground the actor supports himself on the left leg, foot squarely planted on the ground but with a slight bend at the knee. The right leg, bent at the knee, is thrust forward poised on the toes. The body is inclined forward with the right arm bent at right angles to the body and the right index finger pointing at the ground beyond the right foot. The bent left arm is raised across the body so that the left hand is at the level of the actor's chin and above the right

---

not on record. Only his legend lives on, while his likeness is preserved in a famous painting, *Thirteen Celebrated Actors of the T'ung Kuang period* (1862-1908), painted by Shen Yung-p'u and preserved in the theatrical museum in Peking.

Equally few facts seem to be on record for Liu Kan-san. He was a native of Tientsin and is reputed to have received a good education in his youth. He trained under several well-known actors when he joined the famous San Ch'ing troupe of Peking. Later he was a member of the *Ssu-hsi pan.* One of the roles he made famous was that of Liu the go-between in *Picking Up the Jade Bracelet.* Included in his repertoire was a piece called *A Visit to Town Relatives* in which he rode his pet donkey onto the stage in his interpretation of an old peasant woman, much to the delight of the audiences of his day. He trained the animal himself and according to one account he was very attached to his pet. Liu Kan-san left behind him the reputation of a wit who did not scruple to crack at those in high places. It is said that he was imprisoned and flogged during the period of the Sino-Japanese war (1894-95) for his satiric references on stage to the minister Li Hung-chang. He is reputed to have died as a result of this treatment although there is little on record about this or the date of his death. Once more there remains only the legend which has survived among theater people. Liu Kan-san is portrayed in the same painting as Yang-san.

hand, with the left index finger pointing in line with the right index finger.

From this position the actor can swing round to a second stance so that he is standing supported on his right foot squarely on the ground while his bent left leg is raised at waist height. The right arm is bent at shoulder height with the index finger of the right hand pointing directly above the actor's head. The bent left arm is held against the knee of the raised left leg with the left index finger pointing directly to the ground. The shoulders in this case are inclined to the left slightly, the head is bent with the eyes directed to focus on the pointing left hand. From this position the actor can move back into the first position, but with the difference that in this case his left arm is crooked at the elbow and his left hand placed on his waist and the shoulders tilted yet more sharply towards the right as a result of this posture.

When pointing to the left, the actor supports himself on his right leg, which is slightly bent, and the left leg is bent at the knee and poised on the toes. The head is turned right, both arms bent at the elbow are lifted at chest height, the left index finger is pointing left away from the body, and the right index finger points in line with the left and across the body.

When pointing to the front, the actor leans forward from the waist, supporting himself on his right leg, the foot of which is planted firmly on the ground to the rear. The left leg, bent at the knee, is poised on the toes about twelve inches in front of the left foot. Both arms, bent at the elbows, are raised at chest height with the index finger on each hand pointing directly ahead, the eyes focused on the pointing hands.

In the play *The Drunken Yamen Runner,* described previously, the actor performs the following sequence of movements to represent his state of complete intoxication at one point of his meandering across the stage. He starts from a posture in which he stands facing obliquely right, feet well apart, knees slightly bent, arms extended straight down by his side, right shoulder higher than the left, and the torso inclined left. He then turns to face front stage in the same stance with the difference that both hands are raised at shoulder height, thumb held against the forefinger of each hand, palms exposed, head tilted upward, mouth open, and eyes narrowed trying to focus above. The torso is tilted backwards a little to complete the posture known as "drunken peering." Next he moves into a position in which the left foot is squarely on the ground, the right leg bent at the knee is thrust forward poised on the toes. The torso is inclined forwards from the waist, the right arm is extended straight down the side of the body while the left arm crooked at the elbow is thrust forward with the fingers loosely curled over. The head is turned right and in line with the forward tilt of the body. This constitutes the preliminary for another posture called "unable to set out." The actor now faces front stage. Both knees are bent, the left foot is firmly on the ground to the rear, the right leg is thrust forward poised on the toes. Both arms, bent at the elbows, are raised with exposed palms; the fingers are loosely held together but the thumb of each hand is extended downwards. The right arm is held in position directly above the right leg, while the left arm is inclined across the chest towards the right arm. The torso is inclined forward from the waist, left shoulder higher than the right and the head turned in the direction of the hands. From this position the actor swings round obliquely to the right, supported on his right foot, the left leg bent at the knee lifted at waist height and the left foot directed towards the right. The left arm is extended slightly with the left index finger pointing to the left; the arm is bent at the elbow. The right arm, bent at the elbow, is raised to chest height with the right index finger pointing directly towards the sky. The torso and head are inclined slightly towards the right, the left shoulder being higher than the right. At this point the actor comes down from a high to a low posture so that he is bent forward over the waist; both knees are bent with the right foot placed well to the rear and the left foot directed to the front, taking the full weight of the inclined torso. The left arm is extended in a line to the rear with the left index finger pointing in that direction. The right arm, bent at the elbow, is thrust forward from the torso and the head is inclined towards the right. Straightening himself once more, the actor faces front stage; both knees are bent, the right foot well to the rear, the left leg planted squarely forward. The torso is inclined towards the front; the right arm bent at the elbow is held loosely forward with the palm of the hand downwards and the thumb extended. The left arm is held in an identical position but closer in to the torso. Now comes the high climax of the sequence as the actor drops to the ground on his right knee, supported on both hands, which are placed squarely on the ground. His head and shoulders are strained forward over his hands; his eyes are focused on the ground. His back and left thigh are in a straight line, but his left leg, bent at the knee, is cocked over towards the audience so that the sole of his left shoe is fully exposed beneath the hem of his robe, which conceals the rest of his limbs. Urging himself to rise, the drunken yamen runner from this position only succeeds in falling flat on his back, where he remains for a moment like an overturned beetle. His head is raised off the ground; he is supported on his elbows; his forearms are raised with both palms of the hand open and directed towards the sky. His lifted right leg is bent at the knee, the toes directed forward. The left leg, also bent at the knee, is raised a good eighteen inches above the right leg with the left foot directed upwards and slightly to the rear as the drunken man gazes helplessly beyond his raised hands. The sequence of movements described here is interwoven with a drunken soliloquy.

COSTUME

The comic actor works with a wardrobe designed to meet the specific requirements of his role without deviating from the main basic patterns used in the other roles. In general it could be said that the comic actor's costumes tend to be less spectacular, and there is a greater preponderance of simple blue and black cotton materials symptomatic of the humble roles played. In the old days, Chinese society was bound by strict codes of etiquette and social ritual extending into every area of daily life, including the wearing of clothes. A man dressed according to what he was and where he ranked in society, and no one would ever have disputed the necessity for this custom. Not unnaturally, this principle operated in even bolder measure on the stage, although the Chinese stage wardrobe is far less complex than it first seems by virtue of the number of standard patterns of garments and head dresses which can be used in different combinations to suit the particular occasion. Stage costumes are of course made in many different patterns and colors for the most part symbolic, but these are rather rigidly laid down so that order reigns even in this area.

A number of stage garments are multi-purpose in function, and smaller troupes are always happy to take advantage of this fact provided there is no transgression of the basic principles of rank, status, and sex.

A good example of multi-purpose function is seen in the white silk pleated skirt which is a basic article of stage dress for women characters. It is often worn by the comic actors folded and bustled up round the waist to form an apron when playing the roles of servants, wine shop keepers, woodcutters, and the like. The ubiquitous *hsieh-tzu,* or informal robe, although made in several colors, has the same basic cut and is used in many different roles both as an outer and inner garment. It is ankle length with wide sleeves and has an open neck with crossover lapels and a right-hand side fastening. It is an indispensable article in the comic actor's wardrobe.

Several of the important costumes worn both in official and informal

capacities have been described in some detail in the preceding volumes.
Allowing for changes in pattern and color, the basic styles of these robes
for the male roles are used by the comic actors. Important examples are
shown in the photographs (Plates 1-9). Descriptions of the costumes
worn by the two comic characters who appear in the plays translated
here now follow. They are worn without change the whole time they
are on stage.

Liu the go-between. This is a more or less true-to-life costume as it
would have been worn by women of this class. The hair style, shown in
the drawing, is a wig reproducing the coiffure worn by lower class,
middle-aged women of Peking earlier in the century. The wide-sleeved

Drawing 3. Hair style for the *ch'ou-p'o* roles

knee length robe, known as *nü ta-kua,* is also a faithful copy of a dress
style common among ordinary Chinese women during the nineteenth
century and prior to the founding of the Republic in 1912. It is usually
made in a maroon or deep lilac color with a very broad black border to
the cuffs of the sleeves and running round the neckline and hem of the
garment, the black border being reinforced by a narrower white border.
Sometimes the black border on the sleeves is replaced with a broad black

band between two white bands which circle the sleeves three-quarters of the way up from the cuffs. This robe is worn with the wide black silk or cotton Chinese trousers, in this case bound in tightly at the ankles with tapes, over thick white cotton stockings. Black cotton slipper-style shoes with flat white soles of reinforced cotton felt are used, although the more decorative type in coloured satin with embroidered patterns can also be worn. The plain black cotton shoe, however, has become almost universal in more recent and economical times. A broad white silk sash is worn bound round the trousers and the two ends of this hang down beneath the hem of the robe in front. In her hand Liu the go-between carries a long tobacco pipe which has a thin bamboo stem, a brass mouthpiece, and a minute brass bowl. This is often mistaken for an opium pipe, which in fact had a different construction. Tobacco smoking was quite common among Chinese women of this kind, and old countrywomen could often be seen with their tobacco pipes until quite recent times.

The make-up of Liu the go-between is an exception to the customary white paint make-up of the comic actor. It is perfectly naturalistic with perhaps a dab of rouge on the cheeks and a touch of black round the eyes, suggesting a bedizened old harridan.

Ch'ung Kung-tao. The costume of the old warder in the second play represents the dress of a petty official of the *yamen* in the nineteenth century. It is a composite affair which is based on theatrical needs rather than minute historical accuracy. The black hat with its broad upturned brim and scarlet silk floss tassel radiating from the apex of the crown was indeed based on a style used by minor officials in the nineteenth century. In the most elaborate productions the old warder wears the *tsao-li i,* the robe worn by court runners which has been fully described in the second volume. Wide black trousers, silk or cotton, were worn with this garment and tucked into *kuan-hsüeh,* the high black satin boots worn in the male roles with thick white reinforced soles, which, in the case of the comic role described here, are about an inch thick as against the several inches characteristic of the boots worn in the other roles. Once more this is a replica of what was once official footwear. Round the waist the old warder wears a *luan-tai,* a stiff sash, four inches wide with tasselled ends usually plain orange colored or blue and yellow stripe pattern in this role. The comic actor more than any other role perhaps improvised to some extent with his costume and it was not unknown for the actor in a smaller troupe to substitute the ordinary blue *hsieh-tzu* for the *tsao-li i* with his wide black trousers tucked into calf

崇
公
道

Drawing 4. Ch'ung Kung-tao

length cotton white stockings worn with the ordinary black cotton slipper, as seen in the drawing of Ch'ung Kung-tao.

Chinese theatrical costumes, *hsing-t'ou,* were notable for the richly
embroidered fine quality silks and satins used in some of the more
spectacular garments. Each troupe had its own wardrobe, and the more
famous the troupe of course the more luxurious the costumes. Until
1949 it was the practice of leading actors and actresses to have their
personal wardrobes and some of the great performers were noted for
the richness of their stage dress. After 1949 this practice was discouraged
and there was a noticeable move towards austerity of materials in the
stage wardrobe, accompanied by a greater attention to the costumes of
supernumeraries and some of the minor roles which had tended to go
unheeded in the post-war years. Today the colorful costumes of the old
theater have been replaced entirely by a stage wardrobe devised only to
express the tenets of "social realism."

MAKE-UP

A notable feature of the make-up of the traditional comic actor is the
use of the mat white patch painted over the nose and round the eyes and
cheeks in varying shapes and proportions. The white paint is usually embellished with various markings in black and red which differ for each
individual role, although how and when these role markings developed no
one seems able to explain. It is possible that some of them were the in-
ventions of individual actors and became generally used over a period of
time. Chinese authorities list as many as sixty of these white face make-
ups which were regularly used by the comic actors of the *k'un-ch'ü* and
ching-hsi theaters. There were exceptions to the white face make-up; Liu
the go-between is one example. In portraying one unique character who
used to be seen on the Peking stage, Chu Pa-chieh, the mythological pig
character from the celebrated *Journey to the Western Regions,* the
comic wears a pig mask with an articulated lower jaw and ears that flap.
In spite of such exceptions the white paint make-up is so commonly
used that it might justly be called the trademark of the comic actor.

Beards and mustaches are worn in a number of the comic roles; these
may be black or white, colors symbolic respectively of youth or age, as
might be expected. The old warder in *A Girl Setting Out for Trial,* for
example, wears a white beard, which is made in two long narrow wisps
hanging down from either ear, and a straggly mustache, which divides
into two and covers the mouth. The hair is supported on a thin, bent,
metal frame which fits over the ears like spectacles and rests against the

upper lip. Another style of beard favored by the comic actor has a drooping mustache, a short "imperial" constructed to dangle below the chin, and sometimes two wisps from the ears. It is worn by comic actors playing officials, both corrupt and stupid, and is used in conjunction with the hard double-crowned hat with fins protruding at the rear described in the previous volumes. A mustache much used in some *wu-ch'ou* roles has two bristling upturned ends rather like an exaggerated version of the mustache worn by the German kaiser in the first World War. There is another mustache, if it can be called such, consisting of one long stiff, pointed wisp of hair which protrudes absolutely horizontally from the actor's top lip. All mustaches and beards whatever their nature are attached to the kind of wire frame described above.

Some typical hand gestures used by the bewhiskered comic actor are as follows. When he is deep in thought or moved by sudden recognition, the actor holds the bottom of his beard with the thumb and first and second fingers, moving them round in a circular motion. Wearing a mustache, the comic actor twiddles the ends with the thumb and first finger of each hand, palm towards the face but turned sharply outward at the conclusion of each movement, expressing anger or annoyance. When he wears the beard with the dangling portion beneath the chin, a commonly seen gesture consists of holding one hand forward with open fingers and allowing the beard to rest on the upturned palm. Another commonly seen movement when the actor wears the longer style of beard is to sweep both hands with up-turned palms and open fingers down the whole length of the whiskers.

The beard was a theatrical convention used to symbolize a character's disposition and was not necessarily indicative of age, although this was of course also a function of hirsute make-up. For example, a strong, vigorous, and youthful character might wear a full beard in token of his manly qualities where an older character in the same play might have no beard at all. As in all facets of stage practice, theatrical expediency was the issue that mattered. In the case of the comic actors, beards and mustaches were largely used to reinforce qualities of evil, stupidity, and the vacuity of old age.

On the Chinese stage today, characters are noticeably clean-shaven except for the short military toothbrush mustache which has become almost a necessary symbol for the current stage villain, the oppressive landlord or the collaborator with foreign aggressors, who has replaced the type of character once interpreted through the catalystic presence of the clown.

Plate 1. Mei Lan-fang and Hsiao Ch'ang-hua in *A Girl Setting Out for Trial*

Plate 2. The old warder and Su-san (a scene from a Peking production of the 1950s)

Plate 3. The Drunken Yamen Runner (a k'un-ch'ü comic actor)

Plate 4. The actor Wang Te-k'un in the role of Chang San-lang, a man haunted by the ghost of a murdered woman

Plate 5. The actor Hsiao Ch'ang-hua in the role of an evil official

Plate 6. The actor Wang Te-k'un in the role of Chiang Kan, a stupid official of the Three Kingdoms period

Plate 7. The actor Wang Te-k'un in the role of Liu the go-between

Plate 8. The make-up for a comic scholar role

Plate 9. The actor Hsiao Ch'ang-hua teaching students of the comic roles in the Peking training school during the 1950s

Picking Up the Jade Bracelet

Shih yü-cho

Persons in the Play

SUN YÜ-CH'IAO, the pretty daugher of Widow Sun (a hua-tan role)
FU P'ENG, a handsome young bachelor (a hsiao-sheng role)
LIU MEI-P'O, a professional marriage go-between (a ch'ou-p'o role)

The characters are listed in the order of their appearance.

Time: Ming period during the reign of the Emperor Cheng Te (A.D. 1506-21).

About the Play

Picking Up the Jade Bracelet, or simply *Picking Up the Jade,* as it was known among the Chinese theatergoers, was originally the seventh scene in the Peking-style version of a play called *Fa-mên ssu, At the Temple of Buddhist Doctrine.* The Chinese title, incidentally, is an example of ambiguity in word-meaning used to catch the playgoer's ear. The word *ssu* means temple but it can also mean Imperial eunuch, the written character and the spoken tone being the same for either meaning, and the chief eunuch[1] of the Empress, who appears in the twenty-first scene, provides a reason for an important part which used to be played by the leading "painted face role" actors.

Fa-mên ssu had twenty-nine scenes in all and a cast of more than fifty characters. This sounds like a very long play, as indeed it was, although some scenes were quite short, and as scenes on the Chinese stage were recognized by the entry and exit of characters and musical signals only, there were none of the elaborate changes required between scenes as in our own theater. One scene followed another in a constant flux of movement and sound, and in the same way, each play followed the other, there being several in a single program and no curtain between.

---

1. Eunuchs were established members of the Court entourage in Imperial China and they attained great power behind the scenes in Palace circles during the Ming dynasty. They had their own hierarchy and became notorious for their political scheming and control of affairs to a degree far beyond their original functions as attendants on the women of the Imperial court.

It was this that sometimes caused people in the past to think that Chinese plays were of gargantuan length. Nevertheless, *Fa-mên ssu* was devised in days when playgoing was a more leisurely affair for audiences whose dramatic appetites had to be satisfied by catering in full measure to their appreciation of acting form. Ordinary Chinese playgoers welcomed any dramatic material that gave scope to the technical virtuousity of their stage favorites. The actor in performance riveted their attention, and a fully rounded display of skill by some master actor more than compensated for plays which, by our own standards of dramatic tension and plot progression, might seem singularly lacking in interest. One of the great attractions of *Fa-mên ssu* was the fact that it provided the wherewithal for a display of every style of acting practised by exponents of the four main role categories and their subcategories.

The full story of *Fa-mên ssu* is unlikely either to add to or detract from understanding *Picking Up the Jade Bracelet*, which stands entirely on its own theatrical merits, but for reference purposes the plot is outlined in full in the footnote below.[2] Its ingredients are foul murder,

2. The complete plot of *Fa-mên ssu:* After old Liu the go-between arrives home from her adventure, she tells everything to her pork-butcher son, a man of low intelligence. He takes the embroidered slipper from his mother and meeting on the street the young hero for whom it is intended tries to blackmail him, but is stopped by the local constable. In a furious rage the butcher goes off threatening reprisals. A few nights later, armed with his butcher's knife, he goes stealthily to Widow Sun's cottage, where he finds the door ajar. Hearing voices inside, which he mistakes for those of the two lovers, he creeps inside, despatches his victims in the dark, and cutting off the head of one of them, goes and tosses it over the wall of the constable's house. The constable, hearing the noise, comes out and is terrified at the gruesome object lying in front of him. Fearful that he might be accused of the murder he seizes the head and hurls it down his well. Just as he does so a young boy in his service appears and, seeing what is going on, gives a cry of alarm. Losing his nerve completely, the constable pushes the lad down the well also to get rid of any witness of his deed and then reports to the boy's father that his son has decamped, taking some belongings of his master with him. The affair is reported to a magistrate who, as so frequently turns out on the stage, is not a shining example of judicial integrity. He orders the boy's father to pay a fine of ten ounces of silver. As the old man is unable to find the money, Ch'iao-ch'iao, his virtuous daughter, goes to jail as hostage for her father.

Arrived in jail, she finds her fellow inmates are the young lovers of *Picking Up the Jade* episode, accused as responsible for the pork butcher's crime. The two girls soon become confidants; Fu P'eng, the young hero, agrees to pay the fine for Ch'iao-ch'iao's father; and the girl is released, swearing to see justice done for the others. She straight away invites Liu the go-between to dinner, plies her generously

bribery, corruption, and the miscarriage of justice. In the end all wrongs are righted, the guilty are punished, and true love is rewarded by direct intervention of the Empress, who is a character in the play. She not only unites the two lovers we meet in *Picking Up the Jade Bracelet*, falsely accused as accomplices to murder, but simultaneously rewards the hero with the hand of the girl to whom he was betrothed in childhood and who, by one of those coincidences dear to the Chinese playgoer, was instrumental in enabling justice to be done. Although polygamy was accepted in traditional Chinese society by means of concubinage, Imperial authorization of two wives of equal status must have been a novelty even for seasoned Chinese theater fans.

The action of the play takes place during the reign of the Ming Emperor Cheng Te, A.D. 1506-21. The sensationalism of its theme suggests an affinity with the material of the storyteller, who has left his unmistakable imprint on so much of the traditional theatrical repertoire.

---

with wine, and finally gets the whole story out of her. She immediately informs her father, who writes out a detailed plaint based on the facts she has learned. Hearing the Empress Dowager is going to worship at the Fa Men temple, accompanied by her chief eunuch, Ch'iao-ch'iao decides to present the plaint to the Empress herself. Arrived at the temple the chief eunuch tries to turn the girl away, but the Empress insists on hearing her story. As a result she orders her chief eunuch to bring all the principal characters involved in the case before the court. The eunuch obeys her command and the whole story is uncovered. The guilty ones are sent to the supreme court at Peking where the chief eunuch presides over the hearing with the magistrate. The guilty are sentenced, the pork butcher and the constable are executed, and Liu the go-between is sent into exile. As a final gesture, the Empress issues an edict allowing Fu P'eng, his character cleared, to take both Yü-ch'iao and Ch'iao-ch'iao as wives, both to have equal status. While polygamy was sanctioned in Confucian China by allowing concubines to be legally taken into the household, nevertheless wife and concubine were two people apart, and the wife, in theory at least, held the principal authority. A man who tried to make a concubine his wife while his legal wife was alive was liable to the penalty of one hundred strokes with a bamboo stick; conversely if he tried to make his lawful wife into a concubine the same penalty applied. The verdict of the Empress at the end of this play created an unusual marriage situation even by Chinese standards and doubtless gave cause for chatter among the audiences of long ago.

This improbable and tortuously gruesome plot emphasizes what was said earlier about popular dramatic themes smacking of lurid journalism rather than high literature. Nevertheless, such themes provided plenty of scope for the actors and that was the important thing. It must be remembered also that many of the details of this plot were left to the playgoer's imagination rather than realistic portrayal on the stage, where, in any case, everything was acted out with a high degree of symbolism and convention.

His influence is one reason why a play consists of a series of episodes rather than a tightly structured adherence to a central theme, and why subjects often seem more reminiscent of sensational journalism than higher art. The storyteller was in fact the sensational journalist of his day, an entertainer ever ready to use whatever served his purpose for holding the attention of a largely illiterate public.

The factual history of the play seems obscure, possibly because the main thread is lost among that tortuous process of development and counterdevelopment resulting from the impact of numerous regional styles of theater upon each other. Dialect differences, local folklore and musical patterns, variations arising from oral transmission, and the influence of traveling troupes as sponsors of dramatic innovations are some of the factors which have complicated issues. Versions of this play or scenes from it were performed on the regional stages in different provinces, each having its own distinctive local culture and dialect, a further example of the cross-influences at work. The Peking theater was no less subject to them. Political-social trends encouraged the growth of the Peking-style theater as a burgeoning expression of popular culture during the nineteenth century. Its unique style grew out of a public demand for acting virtuosity rather than literary aestheticism on the city stage. Peking audiences readily accepted the innovations introduced by outstanding regional performers, whose theatrical styles in turn were often influenced by the methods of other regions than their own. *Fa-mên ssu* was the kind of material which nourished this theatrical mobility, and like many other pieces, it became fragmented into scenes independent of the main text. This quite common practice was made possible by the inherent structure of Chinese plays together with the fact that audiences concerned primarily with the finer points of acting form remained unperturbed by any lack of plot sequence.

Among the several scenes from this play which achieved isolated performance perhaps none acquired a more enduring popularity than *Picking Up the Jade Bracelet,* not only in Peking but in several regional areas. It was a particular favorite in Kwangsi province, where the local dramatic style was called *k'uei-ch'ü,* and was performed in the provinces of Hunan, Swatow, and Canton as well. During the late Ch'ing period the Anhui style of theater was also introduced into Kwangsi, adding yet further dimensions to this regional form.

Be that as it may, *Picking Up the Jade Bracelet* has long been a popular item of the Kwangsi repertoire and received new acclaim when it was restaged by well-known Kwangsi artists at the First All China Festival of

Traditional and Regional Dramas held in Peking at the end of 1952.
Prior to the systematic relegation of the traditional theater's repertoire, which was one effect of the Cultural Revolution, *Picking Up the Jade* was staged by several troupes which were sent to perform outside China in accordance with official cultural policies of the period. They were the troupe which visited Australia and New Zealand in 1956, the troupe which traveled to Europe (though its tour was cut short) in 1958, the troupe which toured Canada in 1960, the Shanghai Youth Troupe which performed in Hongkong in 1962, and the Visiting Peking City Troupe which also performed in Hongkong in 1963. In each case the inclusion of *Picking Up the Jade Bracelet* on the program was an indication of the measure of its acceptability to both Chinese and foreign audiences. Certainly the combination of pure mime and comic acting made it the unfailing attraction it had always been on the Peking stage. There, the grace, precision, and pure rumbustiousness when three master performers played this lighthearted piece continually endeared it to the hearts of the playgoers. Indeed, such was its perennial appeal that it became a kind of party piece for a whole generation of amateur actresses good, bad, and indifferent!

The main theme of the play as it was adhered to in all its regional variations is as follows. Fu P'eng, a young gentleman of good family (an undisputed qualification for any stage lover of this kind) was out strolling and went by the cottage of Widow Sun. At the door sat her pretty daughter embroidering silk slippers, the widow herself being absent at the Buddhist temple. Immediately smitten by the girl's charms, the young man commenced a flirtation. Equally smitten but dutifully mindful of the decorous conduct enjoined on young women by Chinese etiquette, the girl retired indoors. Not to be outdone, the would-be lover placed a jade bracelet on the ground outside the door and retired to await events. The girl, Yü-ch'iao, unable to contain herself any longer peeped out of doors to see where the admirer had gone and spying the bracelet hastily grabbed it and placed it on her wrist admiringly, just in time to be confronted to her utter confusion by the sudden reappearance of her admirer. Bursting into delighted laughter, he went off announcing to the world that he was going to ask his mother to arrange a formal betrothal.

In the meantime the whole sequence of events had been secretly observed by wily old mama Liu, a professional marriage go-between with an eye to the main chance. Pretending to make a friendly call on the girl, she cross-questioned her. The girl, all innocence at first, was finally tricked into revealing the jade bracelet, which she had desperately tried to conceal. After an angry scene the jubilant go-between extracted the whole story of the flirtation from the girl. Cowed into submission, the girl finally begged mama Liu to help her professionally, which was exactly what the old shrew had intended to happen. She demanded that the girl give her an embroidered slipper to take to the young man as a proof of her authority to meddle in his affairs. Armed with this token, she went off, but not before Yü-ch'iao, unable to curb her amorous anticipation, had badgered the go-between to return in an indecently short space of time according to the rules of procedure, in order to get an immediate offer of marriage. On this note the play ends.

After 1949 some changes were made in the play, particularly in the case of mama Liu, who was transformed into an inquisitive old busybody instead of the scheming old hag she was originally. It is understandable how this play offended contemporary susceptibilities in the context of today's new social attitudes in China. In these translations, however, the concern has been to record the popular theater of China as it was, warts and all, and not as later the reformers decided it ought to be.

Picking up the Jade Bracelet

*The action takes place inside and outside the cottage of the widow
Sun, and the audience is privy to what goes on in both areas simultaneously. There is no fourth wall here; indeed there is no wall at all;
everything is subordinate to the stark purity of theatrical communica-
tion. The stage is empty except for a small table and two chairs, both
table and chairs being covered with embroidered satin cloths. There is
a curtain as a backdrop, with entry right stage and exit left stage, i.e.,
respectively left and right of the audience.*

*The orchestra is seated left stage, i.e., right of the audience. A small
gong is struck. Two gongs are used in the stage orchestra, a large and
small, for major musical accompaniment, and the small version is used
to announce the entry of an actor or actress playing the women's roles.
The mellow but reverberating note of the small gong, whose percussive
pattern varies according to the particular musical style and therefore
dramatic occasion being served, has an anticipatory quality in this case
marked by a double beat, tai, tai. Sun Yü-ch'iao now enters right stage,
i.e., left of the audience, with the mincing step of the hua-tan performer.
She carries a large silk handkerchief in her right hand and both hands
are swung from side to side across the front of her body as she walks
to down right center, i.e., to the front of the stage at a point a little to
the left of the audience. Here she stands for a few seconds glancing
coyly right and left while adjusting the ornaments in her coiffure, a
purely formalized choreographic gesture, before moving to down stage
center, i.e., the central point of the stage directly in front of the audi-*

ence. Obviously an entry pattern of this kind must be adjusted according to the size of the stage, which in China might have been anything between ten feet in length and thirty or more with proportionate discrepancies in depth. It was always enlightening to see the aplomb with which Chinese actors adjusted movement patterns and stage compositions without turning a hair, to meet the given circumstances.

Arrived at the center of the stage, she intones the introductory lines called yin-tzu, generally two or four in number, although in this case there are three lines.

SUN YÜ-CH'IAO:

>   Melancholy, sad of countenance,
>   Busily sewing,
>   I choose my embroidery threads[3]
>   (*Following these words she turns to walk up center; i.e., with her back to the audience she goes to the rear of the stage and seats herself on a chair which the stage attendant has placed in front of the table. Once seated, she begins to recite the poetic lines called shih which customarily follow the yin-tzu and serve to summarize a situation for the audience.*)
>   Tears dampen my silk sleeves,
>   Sorrow multiplies sorrow,
>   The bright spring passes too soon
>   For a shy maiden unlucky in life.
>   (*Relapses into colloquial speech.*)
>   I am the humble Sun Yü-ch'iao.
>   My father died young,
>   Leaving his wife and daughter alone.

3. Every Chinese girl in the past was expected to learn the art of embroidery and become skilled in reproducing design motifs such as plum blossom, symbolizing happiness, peonies symbolizing abundance and wealth, pairs of dragons and phoenix symbolizing *yang* and *yin,* i.e., the husband and wife relationship and many other patterns beloved of Chinese tradition. By the time she reached marriageable age every girl reckoned to have completed a trousseau of clothes, shoes, and other articles of attire, all embroidered by her own hand. The shoes used by women with bound feet were minute articles with pointed toes, flat soles and a slight elevation at the heel. Shoes used in more emancipated times, both in everyday life and on the stage, were slipper style in embroidered satin and with flat soles made of reinforced layers of compressed cotton.

These facts explain the significance of the shoe embroidering scene in *Picking Up the Jade Bracelet.* It represented a customary occupation of a young unmarried girl, a ritual of everyday life translated into theatrical terms.

We make a living selling a few chickens.
Early today mother went to a Buddhist service
And there's no sign of her return.
Very well, I'll go and sit at the open door
And get on with my embroidery.
*(She rises and goes to down center, i.e., to the front of the stage
facing the audience at the central point, where she mimes unbolting
the door, peeping outside, and stepping over the threshold. She
next moves to down right center, a little to the left of the audience
where she pantomimes letting the chickens out of their coop, shooing them into order, and then feeding them by scattering corn
which she has gathered up into the corner of her apron, a garment
she actually wears. This particular sequence has been embellished
by different performers in their time. The actresses especially have
liked to linger over this scene with added touches like wiping the
eyes free of dust from the chaff and so on to the constant approval
of the audience. The chickens fed, the actress returns to down
center where she mimes crossing the threshold before returning to
up center, her original starting point where she takes hold of the
chair and carries it to down center as the preliminary to another
mime sequence lovingly anticipated by the fans. It goes without
saying that everything until now has been performed without
benefit of properties except for the table and chairs; acting skill
and the imaginations of the audience have done the rest. But at
this point some small properties are introduced, a basket contain-
ing a slipper in process of being embroidered and a book of skeins
of embroidery thread (the skeins being left to the imagination),
the whole conveniently placed on the table at the rear by the stage
attendant. Walking over to the table, the actress returns to down
center and seats herself on the chair, placing her basket on the
ground and taking up the slipper and the book of threads. She
then crosses her left leg over her right (only the hua-tan role
players and the comic actors can assume this posture) and begins
an elaborate sequence of pantomime. Taking out the skeins of
thread one by one, she matches them against the material of her
slipper. When the color is finally chosen she draws out a single
thread and drapes it over her shoulder. Replacing the skein in the
book and the book in the basket, the actress then gropes with her
right hand for her needle which is stuck in the chignon of her
coiffure, making the expressive grimace of anguish that only the*

hua-tan can contrive, as she pricks her finger on the needle. Stick-
ing the needle in the top of her apron, she then begins to prepare
the thread, pointing the end, smoothing it, and testing it between
her teeth, audibly assisted by a twanging string in the orchestra,
before she begins the actual process of stitching the shoe, in which
process she is busily engaged when the hero appears on the scene.
Again this mime sequence is elaborated or shortened according to
stage circumstances and the judgement of the performer.)

SUN YÜ-CH'IAO (*sings in nan pang-tzu*):
  It was bad luck my father died early,
  Leaving mother and daughter to strive alone.
  Deserted and lonely I restrain my rising tears.
  (*Fu P'eng enters up right, i.e., the entry at the rear of the stage to*
  the left of the audience. He carries a fan in his right hand and his
  left sleeve is flung outward and then upward to the waist in broad
  sweeps in time to his gait. His steps are wide, each foot being drawn
  up to the other before moving forward so that there is almost a
  crab-like motion with the stiffly extended legs. In costume and
  deportment he represents the archetypal young hero of good
  family and education as conceived on the old Peking stage. He
  sings in nan pang-tzu, a musical style largely used for the young
  hero roles and for women.)

FU P'ENG: Here am I, Fu P'eng, strolling at leisure.
  As the prospect seems less pleasing at this side of the street,
  I'll go by way of Widow Sun's house.
  (*This action is indicated by a few formalized steps and turns em-*
  bracing but two or three feet on a small stage, bringing him in
  front of Yü-ch'iao to stare admiringly. She on her part has seen
  his approach and, though suitably embarrassed, she obviously
  wants to return the young man's glances without seeming to do
  so, to the extent that she becomes flustered and pricks her finger
  with her needle. At his arrival she has risen to her feet and after
  this preliminary flirtation she hurriedly steps inside and bolts the
  door again. Fu P'eng bursts into loud laughter at this point.)
  He, he, he.
  (*The laughter of the hsiao-sheng actor who plays the kind of role*
  depicted here is high-pitched to the point of shrillness with each
  syllable enunciated separately in a controlled and falling cadence
  of sound. Among the many qualities required of the actor of this

particular kind of role a mastery of this special vocal technique was especially appreciated by the seasoned theater goer.

While all this flirtatious by-play has been going on mama Liu the marriage go-between has appeared right stage, i.e., at the rear entry to the left of the audience. She carries a long tobacco pipe in one hand and her costume, hairstyle, and deportment typify a kind of old beldame found in China at the beginning of the century. In some shortened versions of the play Liu the go-between rushes down the center of the stage and scares off the flirting pair. The version given here is somewhat different being one that was staged thirty or forty years ago.)

FU P'ENG *(sings in hsi-p'i yao-pan)*:
The Goddess of the Moon cannot compare with that girl I saw just now.
(He goes off left stage, i.e., to the right of the audience. Liu the go-between moves down stage looking right and left and addresses the audience. She bursts into laughter.)

LIU THE GO-BETWEEN: Such passion makes me smile to see. I'll keep my eye on those two and find out what's going on!
(She hides herself; i.e., she returns to right stage and takes up a position of vantage. The movements of Liu the go-between are controlled as all Chinese stage movement must be, but they are far less conventionalized than those of the other actors, and they are devastating in their representational cunning while carrying the necessary hint of theatrical exaggeration. There is always leeway for a little exaggeration in this role and even a touch of knockabout, although the master actors keep this restrained rather than otherwise.

Sun Yü-ch'iao, who during this interlude has been seated busy with her embroidery, or pretending to be, now mimes unbolting the door once more and peeps cautiously out. She throws the audience a dazzling smile then steps out to sing in hsi-p'i yao-pan.)

SUN YÜ-CH'IAO: My needle faltered when I saw that young gentleman standing there and now my heart is on fire.
(She enters and closes the door again. Liu the go-between hides herself by retreating off stage at the rear as Fu P'eng enters down left stage, i.e., right of the audience.)

FU P'ENG: Ya!
(Sings in hsi-p'i yao-pan.)

This time she will not be able to resist me.

(*He gazes expectantly at the door as he draws the jade bracelet from his sleeve. Sun Yü-ch'iao anxiously opens the door again and cautiously peeps first right and then left where she is overcome with confusion and embarrassment at what she sees while at the same time unable to conceal her interest. Fu P'eng bursts into laughter, again a highly controlled cadence of sound.*)
He, he, he!

(*He sings in hsi-p'i yao-pan.*)
I'll pretend to buy some chickens as a way to start up an acquaintance.

(*Speaks*)
I offer you my respects, young lady.

SUN YÜ-CH'IAO (*with becoming modesty expressed through glance and gesture*):
I am at your service, sir. Can I help you?

FU P'ENG: May I enquire if this is Mrs. Sun's house?

SUN YÜ-CH'IAO: This is indeed my mother's cottage.

FU P'ENG: Have I the honor of addressing the daughter of Mrs. Sun?

SUN YÜ-CH'IAO: May I ask who you are, sir?

FU P'ENG: My family name is Fu, my given name P'eng, my courtesy title Yün-ch'eng.[4] I live in Mei-wu district. I have heard that you have very fine chickens for sale.

SUN YÜ-CH'IAO: My mother is not at home. Our chickens have all been sold. I must ask you to buy somewhere else.

FU P'ENG: In that case I will take my leave.

(*A flirtation[5] is now well under way indicated by glances between*

4. Names: A Chinese personal name consists of two parts, the family name, or *hsing,* and the given name, or *ming.* There is also a courtesy title, or *tzu,* adopted by most educated people and frequently used alone. It is an important means of social identification and expression of personality for the person concerned. When a couple married it was often usual to take a courtesy title for a marriage name. The subject of Chinese nomenclature is far more complicated than even these few facts suggest, but all that need be said here is that in introducing himself in this way the hero in the play was making it clear that he wanted to be accepted as something more than conventional "Mr. Fu," so to speak.

5. Women's deportment: In Confucian China women of good character were strictly segregated from the opposite sex and it was unthinkable that any woman could enter into conversation with a man outside her own family circle of her own accord. In their outward behavior, women were supposed to keep their eyes from roving and modestly focused downwards; they were not supposed to laugh aloud

*the two and by-play indicated by gesture and posture which has
been given different interpretations according to the performers
involved. At a point where they are transfixed by each other's
looks there is a loud cough from Liu the go-between rear stage,
and they both look quickly at the door, imaginary still. Fu P'eng
bursts into laughter:*)

He, he, he.

(*Sings in hsi-p'i yao-pan.*)

I must have this girl, but how to find a way to become intimate
with her. I'll leave this jade bracelet which I have in my sleeve. If
she keeps it I shall know there is hope to make her my bride.
(*He offers the jade bracelet to Sun Yü-ch'iao, who refuses it
vehemently, hurries into the house again, closing the door and then
taking the chair and placing it on the left side of the table, its
original position at the rear of the stage. This of course symbolizes
taking the chair from the courtyard, where she was originally sitting
before the open door, back into the house. Fu P'eng indicating to
the audience that he has reached a decision, places the jade bracelet
carefully on the ground in front of the "cottage." He then strides
off left stage, right of the audience, with another cadence of
laughter as he goes. Next follows the passage of pantomime and
dance which has given the play its title. After Fu P'eng's departure,
Sun Yü-ch'iao, unable to restrain her curiosity, comes down stage
to open the door once more and cautiously comes out to search
at down right stage. Seeing no one, she turns to find the bracelet
at her feet. She then commences a sequence involving great play
with the handkerchief always carried by the hua-tan performer
and used to reinforce hand gesture and facial expression. In this
case it indicates a progressive weakening of the will to resist temptation, a constant retreating and advancing between hesitancy and
desire until the bracelet is finally snatched from the ground. Every
movement and gesture of the performer, though representational*

---

or to show their teeth in a smile or display emotion of any kind before the other
sex. This conservative and restricted demeanor was both symbolized in the stage
technique of the virtuous women roles to a high degree of formalism and on the
other hand debunked in the coquettish *hua-tan* roles such as Yü-ch'iao in this play.
Her flashing smile, wide eyes, flirting behind her handkerchief, exaggerated displays of bashfulness, and inability to conceal her amorous desires, provided a
theatrical catharsis in a society whose everyday lives were attuned to restraint in
every outward manifestation of sex.

in expression, moves through a strictly devised pattern of rhythms enforced by the musical accompaniment. Space is used to the maximum at this point, doors, even imaginary ones, are forgotten as the stage becomes a dance floor. The length and variations in this sequence depend on factors like the size of the stage as well as the particular performer. In more recent times there as been a trend to emphasize the representational mime at the expense of the old choreographic rhythms which undoubtedly demand a polished performer. Amateur actresses, for whom this was a favorite piece, did sometimes tend to draw out the bracelet scene to tedious lengths without a compensatory verve and spirit.

In one version of this scene Sun Yü-ch'iao is just about to screw her courage up to the sticking point and seize the bracelet when Liu the go-between gives one of her ominous coughs from rear stage and Sun Yü-ch'iao leaps away from the jewelry like a startled gazelle. In the most traditional version of this piece, picking up the bracelet concludes with a pure dance climax when Sun Yü-ch'iao, bracelet in left hand and handkerchief in right, expresses her delight in a choreographic celebration which takes her from up left, i.e., the rear of the stage to the right of the audience, in a diagonal line to down right center, i.e., front of the stage left of the audience, an oblique path across the stage. Performing this, she is on her toes moving with short rapid steps, of course to music, her arms swinging gracefully outwards at waist height and then inward with hands just below her chin, elbows bent outwards. Arrived at down right center, she begins to try the bracelet on her wrist with admiring glances just as Fu P'eng strides on from left stage again, i.e., to the right of the audience. She is thoroughly nonplussed and hastily ducks toward the ground, but it is too late to put the bracelet back there and she hurriedly turns to right center and pretends to be shooing her chickens to order. Fu P'eng bursts into laughter, an echoing but controlled cadence of sound:)

FU P'ENG: Excellent!

(*At this point Sun Yü-ch'iao tries to give him back the bracelet. Standing facing the audience, her face is shielded from the young man's gaze by the handkerchief clutched in her upturned right hand as she thrusts the bracelet in her left hand at him with a staccato movement across her body, first under then over the handkerchief, but to no avail. Fu P'eng turns and strides away, singing in hsi-p'i yao-pan.)*

I'll return home immediately and ask my mother to send a marriage go-between to represent the family.

(With a last laugh he exits left stage in a final shrill, dropping away of sound.)

SUN YÜ-CH'IAO: Well!

(Sings hsi-p'i yao-pan.)

I know Fu P'eng's intentions, and now he wants to call a go-between to represent his family.

(She turns and hastily shoos back the few stray chickens; this is done at right center. Then she moves down center and mimes closing the doors, first giving a last glance to right and left before finally shutting the doors and turning to make her exit up left.

Liu the go-between enters down right, i.e., to the left of the audience and turns to address the house from down center, i.e., front stage, gesticulating with the long tobacco pipe held in her right hand.)

LIU THE GO-BETWEEN: What a lark!

(She gives a hoarse cackle of laughter and begins to sing in hsi-p'i chin pan.)

I saw what those two were up to. It's improper though I can hardly stop laughing myself.

(She gives a sudden start as she places the hot bowl of her tobacco pipe to her mouth in error.)

Aiya!

(No English word can suggest the feeling in this very characteristic Chinese interjection especially as it is used by the comic actor. It is short, explicit and contains a world of inference dependent on how it is used. After this set back she addresses herself to the audience again.)

LIU THE GO-BETWEEN: Liu the marriage go-between, that's me. Meaning to say I've earned my living as a matchmaker ever since my old man departed this world leaving one son behind, Liu Pao. He's a pork butcher by trade. We've gone through some pretty hard times, but let's not talk about that. Early this morning I was passing Widow Sun's door when I happened to see that young monkey Fu P'eng trying to fix up a secret tryst with Miss Yü-ch'iao, if you please! But of course they can't get away with that by themselves. There's nothing more to be said, I'll have to go along to Widow Sun's and fix things up for them. That's right and proper, isn't it? Just the thought of it makes me smile, it really does. What a lark!

(*Bursts into a cackle of laughter and sings hsi-p'i yüan-pan mode.*) Yours truly was up bright and early this morning and passing along the street I came across young Fu P'eng trying to fix up a secret tryst with Sun Yü-ch'iao. I saw how things were between them right away, so there's no reason why I shouldn't act as the go-between. I could split my sides laughing. I'll get back to the house and talk things over with them.

(*She exits left stage, i.e., right of the audience.*)

SUN YÜ-CH'IAO (*enters up right and sings in hsi-p'i yüan-pan*):
Early this morning sitting outside sewing, I suddenly saw that young gentleman Fu P'eng come up to the door. He offered me a jade bracelet as a token of his affection. Oh, if only a matchmaker would come along quickly.

(*She sits down on the left-hand chair and takes up her embroidery again.*)

LIU THE GO-BETWEEN: (*enters down right and goes to down center. Sings in hsi-p'i yüan-pan*):
As for me, I came along so early I've had not time to eat break-fast. Well, here we are at Widow Sun's house.

(*Calls out in a loud voice.*)

Open the door!

SUN YÜ-CH'IAO (*from inside*):
Who is it?

LIU THE GO-BETWEEN (*calls out again*):
Do as you're told.

LIU THE GO-BETWEEN (*sings in hsi-p'i yüan-pan*):
It's mama Liu. I'm having a day off.

(*Inside Yü-ch'iao is hurriedly concealing the bracelet by pushing it up her wrist under her sleeve.*)

Hurry up there and open this door.

SUN YÜ-CH'IAO: I'm coming.

(*She slowly opens the door and peeps out to the left.*)

Oh, mama Liu!

LIU THE GO-BETWEEN: Right here!

SUN YÜ-CH'IAO: Oh please come in, mama Liu.

(*Liu the go-between rushes in with almost indecent haste and starts searching in every corner of the room.*)

What are you looking for, mama?

(*She is nervous and embarrassed at the same time, and Liu's nosey attitude has immediately produced an air of agitated flutter on the stage.*)

LIU THE GO-BETWEEN: Looking for?

(*Sings in hsi-p'i yüan-pan.*)

I thought I heard your mother in the next room.

SUN YÜ-CH'IAO: My mother's gone to a Buddhist service.

LIU THE GO-BETWEEN: Oh!

(*Sings in hsi-p'i yüan-pan.*)

If your mother's not at home, could it be somebody else?

SUN YÜ-CH'IAO: Somebody else?

LIU THE GO-BETWEEN (*sings in hsi-p'i yüan-pan*):

Pearls like tears cannot be hidden.

SUN YÜ-CH'IAO (*still uneasy and trying to create a diversion*):

I'll go and bring you some tea.

(*She exits up left.*)

LIU THE GO-BETWEEN: Hurry up then.

(*Singing in hsi-p'i chin-pan.*)

That child's blushes betray her. How does she think that she can fool me with her tricks?

(*With Sun Yü-ch'iao out of the room Liu the go-between begins a frenzied search, turning up the covers of the chairs and table in turn as though her life depended on it. She is in the middle of this frantic display when Sun Yü-ch'iao returns right stage with a tray and a cup of tea. In her anxiety to cover up her behavior, Liu grabs at the cup and burns her hand and jumps a foot in the air.*)

LIU THE GO-BETWEEN: Aiyo!

SUN YÜ-CH'IAO: What's the matter?

LIU THE GO-BETWEEN: Oh, it's nothing.

SUN YÜ-CH'IAO: Please take a seat, mama.

(*They sit down one on either side of the table, Liu in the chair at the left, i.e., right of the audience. She crosses her left leg over her right and leans back nonchalantly, pipe in one hand, but her eyes are roaming.*)

LIU THE GO-BETWEEN: This tea's very fragrant. What kind is it?

SUN YÜ-CH'IAO: It's called heavenly flight.

(*Liu is still searching the room with her eyes, her mind in two places at once.*)

LIU THE GO-BETWEEN: Yo!

(*Pointing to the four corners of the room with her pipe.*)

You don't say, flying in a cottage. I say, girl, are you all right?

SUN YÜ-CH'IAO: I'm all right, mama. What about you?

LIU THE GO-BETWEEN: I'm all right. I say, my dear, who bound your feet for you?[6]

(*She is bending over to look at Sun Yü-ch'iao, who is sitting with one leg cocked over the other showing her tiny foot. Liu is beginning to work up a conversation to serve her purpose at this point.*)

SUN YÜ-CH'IAO: Mother did them.

6. The binding of girls' feet in childhood was a social custom endured by Chinese women for centuries in the cause of fashionable appearance and sex appeal, at least among some classes of society. Authorities are divided on the origins of this practice and dates vary between the fourth and tenth centuries A.D., but it seems generally agreed that it originated with the palace concubines. It may, therefore, presumably be considered as one more curb used in the segregation of women. Be that as it may the custom remained widespread until 1912 when it was forbidden under the new Republic's legislation, although movements had gone on long before, both among Chinese and Western missionary circles, to abolish the custom.

What happened was that the feet were tightly bound with bandages restricting normal growth and resulting in an atrophy of the bone structure that produced a tiny malformed foot as small as two or three inches in the most extreme cases. This caused women to walk with a short teetering step and a swaying from the hips which became a mark of fashionable esteem. The Manchus, who conquered China in the seventeenth century and remained its rulers until the early twentieth century, forbade their own women to bind their feet, and there were certainly some classes of Chinese women who did not do so, particularly those who had to work on the land and on the water. In general, the habit was commonest among the upper and middle classes and the women of the pleasure quarters. What is most relevant to our purpose here is that the custom was perpetuated on the stage where, until very recent times, actors who played the parts of coquettes and similar characters were trained to wear the *ch'iao,* a contraption resembling a small stilt which was bound to the actor's foot, the wooden base being shaped like a small hoof to resemble the form of a bound foot. It entailed walking, running, and fighting *au point* the whole time the actor was on stage. The old style *hua-tan* actors were noted for their skilful display of movement and acrobatics while wearing these accessories which, needless to say, required long years of mastery and had become used by fewer and fewer performers long before 1949 when the practice was dropped from the training curriculum.

LIU THE GO-BETWEEN: Your mother, eh? My, so tiny, they're really three-inch golden lilies.[7]

(Indicating her own feet, which are clad in the flat-soled slippers invariably worn in the comic roles and which are three or four times the size of the simulated bound feet of the hua-tan actress.) Look at mama's feet. See, they're also three inches across inside.

SUN YÜ-CH'IAO: Like my mother.

LIU THE GO-BETWEEN: Like your mother, eh? I say, who did your hair for you?

SUN YÜ-CH'IAO: My mother did that also.

LIU THE GO-BETWEEN: Your mother again, eh? It's beautifully combed. Aiya! That cluster of flowers you're wearing is all crooked.

(Sun Yü-ch'iao puts her right hand up to her hair.)

SUN YÜ-CH'IAO: Oh!

LIU THE GO-BETWEEN: No, this side.

(Sun Yü-ch'iao touches her hair with her left hand and as she does so involuntarily reveals the bracelet on her wrist.)

LIU THE GO-BETWEEN: Ya! I saw it!

SUN YÜ-CH'IAO: What did you see, mama?

(There is a climax of flurry and agitation as she hurriedly tries to conceal the bracelet, but Liu the go-between has achieved her aim and is determined to press the attack home. The two women have risen and move to center stage.)

LIU THE GO-BETWEEN: What's that you have suddenly glistening and gleaming on your wrist there? Mama's eyesight's not too good. What is it?

SUN YÜ-CH'IAO *(forced to confess)*:
    It's a jade bracelet.

LIU THE GO-BETWEEN: But wherever did poor people like you get a thing like that?

SUN YÜ-CH'IAO: I picked it up outside.

---

7. Golden lilies, *chin-lien:* This was a euphemism that passed into usage as a term for describing the bound feet of women. One explanation of the name was that it derived from the words of an emperor of the fourth century A.D. who, on seeing his favorite concubine dance on a lily-embellished stage, exclaimed, "Every footstep makes a lily grow," although it requires a considerable stretch of the imagination to envisage how women danced with bound feet. Presumably, if it indeed happened, it was more akin to stilt walking than anything resembling dancing. Three-inch golden lilies, *san-ts'un chin-lien,* was a common expression of admiration for a woman's appearance in the nineteenth century.

LIU THE GO-BETWEEN: Now, isn't that nice! I was up at four this morning and out all day until six o'clock this afternoon and I didn't pick up a thing!

SUN YÜ-CH'IAO: Your luck was out, mama!

LIU THE GO-BETWEEN: You're right! My luck was out. You might also say it's my age, and you could be right. Now, my dear, let mama have a look at it, eh?

SUN YÜ-CH'IAO: Please do, mama.

(*She hands her the bracelet. Liu the go-between snatches it greedily.*)

Be careful, mama!

LIU THE GO-BETWEEN: Don't you worry; I'll look after it. It's no use; mama's eyesight's failing. I'll look at it outside.

SUN YÜ-CH'IAO: Don't you think I had better go with you?

LIU THE GO-BETWEEN: You really have nothing to worry about. Don't fret yourself; mama's not going to steal it.

(*Bursts into a cackle of laughter and addresses audience.*)

This child's got hold of an imitation jade bracelet and she's frightened I'm going to run off with it.

(*Turning on Sun Yü-ch'iao fiercely.*)

Take it, girl; you're in such a dither you can't even tell whether it's real or imitation.

(*Aggressively.*)

Now tell me where you got it!

SUN YÜ-CH'IAO: I picked it up outside, truly I did!

LIU THE GO-BETWEEN: Oh go on with you! I do believe you have a lover and he gave it to you!

SUN YÜ-CH'IAO (*showing her annoyance*):

I invited you into our house out of hospitality and with the best intentions. Why do you talk in this evil way? If you continue I shall ask you to leave.

LIU THE GO-BETWEEN: Listen to her and her temper! Why fly into a tantrum with me? Tut, tut! I tell you, girl, you can't abuse me like that!

SUN YÜ-CH'IAO: You can talk!

LIU THE GO-BETWEEN: You listen to me!

SUN YÜ-CH'IAO: You can talk!

LIU THE GO-BETWEEN: Be quiet. Listen to me!

(*Singing in hsi-p'i yüan-pan.*)

I got up so early this morning I had nothing to eat. I saw that lad
Fu P'eng, the young monkey, in front of this house announcing
that he wanted to buy chickens, a trick to start up an intrigue. He
left a jade bracelet before the door on purpose. I was right there
on the stage and secretly watched him.
(*Liu the go-between is gesturing and using her pipe clutched in
one hand to emphasize her points. Her whole demeanor is that of
a scold, and Sun Yü-ch'iao is wilting before the onslaught expressed
in a flurry of hand gestures and facial expression. By her reference
to being a witness on the stage Liu reveals the time-honored function
of the clown in keeping theatrical pretension in check. Next follows a kuo-men, a musical interlude performed on the hu-ch'in,
designed to bridge the intervals between the ongoing dialogue of a
play and to accompany any action. In this case, it is a hilarious
reconstruction of Sun Yü-ch'iao's flirtation with the eligible young
stranger, her coy embarrassment, her meaningful glances, finding
of the bracelet, dallying with temptation, and final seizure of the
coveted article leading to the joyful dance which climaxed the
series of events. Nothing is left out, and in the exaggerated mimicry
Liu the go-between never misses the mark. This interlude becomes
not only a parody of a stage character's behavior but of hallowed
stage procedures as they have always been used to simulate that
behavior. The shafts are doubly barbed. As the laughter grows, the
parody becomes a manifestation of the clown's talent for bringing
his audience down to earth. In the words of the Chinese proverb:
"He who weeps at the play distresses himself for the ancients." In
other words, theater is not to be taken seriously. Sun Yü-ch'iao is
crestfallen as Liu the go-between relapses into vigorous speech
again:*)
LIU THE GO-BETWEEN: Deny it if you can, but I saw what you did. I
watched you open the door, and then you and Fu P'eng began to
make eyes at each other. You're all modesty now, but the pair of
you stood and talked half the day! Then young Fu P'eng offered
you the bracelet, but you pretended not to want it so he left it
lying on the ground. You looked around to make sure no one saw
you and then you quickly picked it up. When he came back suddenly you were in a panic and tried to return it to him. Where-
upon Fu P'eng went off, and when you were quite sure he'd gone
you slipped the bracelet on your wrist. You're found out, aren't

you? Now am I making false charges? Trying to put me in the wrong indeed! Let me tell you I was in this business before you were born. You really exasperate me!

(Sings in hsi-p'i yao-pan)

I've had more than enough of this affair.

SUN YÜ-CH'IAO *(she is now contrite and wishes to make her peace with the old girl)*:

Ah, Liu . . .

LIU THE GO-BETWEEN *(interrupting)*:

Liu what? Liu what? Am I a nobody?

SUN YÜ-CH'IAO: Mrs. Liu.

LIU THE GO-BETWEEN: Mrs. Liu, Mrs. Liu. Am I not entitled to respect as an elder?

SUN YÜ-CH'IAO *(kneeling before her in tears)*:

Oh dear, mama Liu . . .

LIU THE GO-BETWEEN: Hm, hm! On your knees, eh? Now look here, tell me if it's true or not! Out with it!

(Sun Yü-ch'iao shakes her head)

LIU THE GO-BETWEEN: It's no use shaking your head; that means nothing. A nod would be more to the point!

(Sun Yü-ch'iao nods her head)

Ah! So mama wasn't wrong after all. Stand up!

(Sun Yü-ch'iao begins to rise, but a cough from the old girl sends her hastily to her knees again.)

Mama's just been pulling your leg. Now get up!

SUN YÜ-CH'IAO: Oh thank you, mama. Please sit down. Well, that's that. As you saw through everything it will be excellent if you can now make all the arrangements.

(They are seated on either side of the table again.)

LIU THE GO-BETWEEN: That's easy. As he's given you a jade bracelet you must send him some precious article in return.

SUN YÜ-CH'IAO: Ours is a poor household. What is there I can send?

LIU THE GO-BETWEEN: Have you any embroidered slippers?

SUN YÜ-CH'IAO: Yes, I have. How many pairs do you want?

LIU THE GO-BETWEEN: I'm not going to open a shoe shop. One will be enough.

SUN YÜ-CH'IAO: Wait a moment, and I'll get one. You shall have it right away, mama.

LIU THE GO-BETWEEN: Hand it over, and I'll keep it safely on your behalf.

SUN YÜ-CH'IAO: I trust you, mama.

LIU THE GO-BETWEEN: Well, I'll be on my way.

(*They rise and begin to move downstage.*)

SUN YÜ-CH'IAO (*anxiously and with a detaining gesture*):
When will you bring back an answer?

LIU THE GO-BETWEEN (*as though suddenly recollecting*):
Oh, that's right; I haven't set a date for you yet! What about one year from now?

SUN YÜ-CH'IAO (*pouting*):
That's much too long!

LIU THE GO-BETWEEN: Half a year then!

SUN YÜ-CH'IAO: Still too long!

LIU THE GO-BETWEEN: Then what about one month?

SUN YÜ-CH'IAO: Make it sooner still!

LIU THE GO-BETWEEN: Sooner still. (*Aside.*) She really can't wait!
Then what about making it three days?

SUN YÜ-CH'IAO: Why three days?
(*Wailing in k'u-pan.*)
Ah, ah, mama Liu, ah!
(*This is a long drawn out cadence of sound rather than song as such, but the rhythmic pattern is formally structured.*)

LIU THE GO-BETWEEN: (*shrugging her shoulders resignedly and singing in hsi-p'i yao-pan*):
I'll take this embroidered slipper as a token and guard it carefully.
(*Relapsing into speech.*)
Right! Now be on the lookout for my return.

SUN YÜ-CH'IAO: Oh indeed, mama, I shall be. Come back without delay!

LIU THE GO-BETWEEN: No need to remind me time and again.

SUN YÜ-CH'IAO: How I long to meet him!

LIU THE GO-BETWEEN: Look for the butterfly when you enter the garden, my girl!
(*They go out through the doorway.*)

SUN YÜ-CH'IAO: I'll see you off, mama!

LIU THE GO-BETWEEN: There's no need. I'll be on my way.

SUN YÜ-CH'IAO (*with detaining hands*):
Mama, wait!

LIU THE GO-BETWEEN: Now what's the matter?

SUN YÜ-CH'IAO: When will you come back with an answer?

LIU THE GO-BETWEEN: (*exasperated*):
Haven't I just told you in three days' time?

SUN YÜ-CH'IAO: I can't wait so long, mama!

LIU THE GO-BETWEEN: I know you can't wait and I'll bring you an
answer as quickly as I can. Now get inside!

SUN YÜ-CH'IAO: If you don't promise I'll lock you inside.

(*She makes a gesture of pushing the annoyed Liu back.*)

LIU THE GO-BETWEEN: What?

SUN YÜ-CH'IAO: I'll bolt the door on you!

LIU THE GO-BETWEEN: Oh, leave me alone, do!

SUN YÜ-CH'IAO: All right, you can go.

LIU THE GO-BETWEEN: I'm delighted! You seem determined to annoy
me with your tomfoolery!

(*Sun Yü-ch'iao turns and makes her exit.*)

LIU THE GO-BETWEEN (*turning to address the audience*):
Look at that minx! She can't even wait three days, though she
won't admit it in so many words. Why, in my young days we
couldn't even wait five minutes!

(*She goes off left stage, i.e., to the right of the audience, who are
given a parting nod and a leer.*)

THE END

A Girl Setting Out for Trial

Nü ch'i-chieh

Persons in the Play

CH'UNG KUNG-TAO, a warder in charge of prisoner escort (a wen-ch'ou role)

A JAILER, *chin-tzu* (a hsiao-ch'ou role)

SU-SAN, a woman prisoner, *fan-fu*, and onetime courtesan and lover of the young scholar Wang Chin-lung (a ch'ing-i role)

A PRISON OFFICIAL, *yü-kuan*, (a hsiao-ch'ou role)

TRAVELER'S VOICE OFF

CHARACTERS WHO ARE NAMED IN THE PLAY BUT DO NOT APPEAR ON STAGE

WANG CHIN-LUNG, also called SAN-LANG, a young scholar-official

SHEN YEN-LIN, a wealthy Shansi merchant who became enamoured of Su-san and secretly paid her ransom as a courtesan to make her his concubine though an unwilling one

P'I-SHIH, the jealous wife of the merchant who poisoned him in error for Su-san on whom she then laid the blame

CH'UN-CHIN, a flirtatious slave girl whom P'i-shih used as her accomplice and go-between

CHAO CHIEN-SHENG, a local scholar who had an affair with the slave girl and was used by her mistress, P'i-shih, to bribe the magistrate

WANG HSIEN-LING, the corrupt local magistrate (not to be confused with Wang Chin-lung)

LI-HU, the official torturer

The characters are listed in the order of their appearance.

Time: early Ming period (A.D. 1506-21).

About the Play

Chinese sources attribute the origins of the play *Jade Pavilion of Happiness*,[1] of which *A Girl Setting Out for Trial* is a part, to a Ming story, *Yü-t'ang ch'un lo nan p'eng fu*, published in a collection called *Ching shih t'ung-yen*. The action of the story is set in the reign of the Emperor Cheng Te, A.D. 1506-21, and is popularly credited as being based on the actual love story of a famous courtesan of that period. The theme was apparently a favorite with the different genres of story-tellers during the reign of the Emperor Ch'ien Lung, 1736-96, as well as of some romantic novelists of the period. There has been speculation among Chinese writers as to whether the stage version came from the storytellers or the novelists. Like so many traditional Chinese plays this one evolved through many different sources and regional versions and where it all first began no one now seems readily able to determine. What can be said with more certainty for our purpose here is that the play as it was first produced on the Peking stage was the creation of the actor Wang Yao-ch'ing, 1882-1954.

Wang's acting career came to an end in 1911 when he lost his singing voice,[2] but he went on to become a great teacher and innovator. He did

1. *Jade Pavilion of Happiness, Yü-t'ang ch'un*, was a romantic analogy used by the young hero in the play of that name to designate his courtesan sweetheart, Su-san.

2. There were two ways for an actor to lose his voice: (a) *tao-tsang*, breaking in male adolescence and (b) *t'a-chung*, the deterioration of vocal powers in maturity. The first occurrence was cause for anxiety on the part of both teachers and promising apprentices in the event their first fine quality was lost, as sometimes happened. In any case, it meant retirement from active performance for a period, and this could be difficult for a training school which often depended on public performances by its senior students to bring in much needed revenue. Complete deterioration of the voice in maturity was a disaster for any actor and frequently came about

a great deal to develop the acting forms and musical style of the women's roles, at that period the absolutely undisputed domain of male performers, including the role of Su-san. Wang was also one of the first teachers to break the taboo on women pupils and he became the instructor of several actresses of great promise. The actor Mei Lan-fang, 1894-1961, was also Wang's private pupil in his youth and he constantly acknowledged his debt to his teacher. Mei modelled his own interpretation of Su-san, a role he made famous during the twenties and thirties, on many of Wang's ideas, and a new generation of actresses carried on this tradition.

From 1922 onwards, Mei was partnered in this play by Hsiao Ch'ang-hua, 1877-1960s, the doyen of comic actors during this century and one who more than any other fixed the image of the old warder Ch'ung Kung-tao in the public's imagination. His interpretation of the knowing, somewhat cynical, but kindly petty official setting about his routine duty but losing his professional indifference at sight of his charge was one the Chinese playgoer relished. As soon as Hsiao made his first entry shaking a reproving finger and rolling his Peking *r*'s, the audience sat back in anticipation, knowing they were in the hands of a master of his genre.

In his memoirs,[3] Mei Lan-fang has made this comment on the old warder's role: "Ch'ung Kung-tao, though a supporting character, is very important. When the two leave the jail for the assizes there is no one else on the stage. Whenever Su-san completes a sung stanza he (Ch'ung) has to discourse. If he says too much the audience is bored; if he says too little the actor who is singing (Su-san) has no time to rest, so it is difficult to perform with exact timing. The *ch'ou* actors who performed with me in the early years were Wang Ch'ang-lin, Li Ching-shan, and in recent years Hsiao Ch'ang-hua. Wang was faithful to the old text but minimized improvisation, at which both Li and Hsiao were excellent. According to theatrical custom, only the *ch'ou,* and the *wen-ch'ou* at that, is allowed to ad lib. The *hua-tan* may also do it. When the comic actor improvizes during performance, he must pun with a straight face and no laughter; his words must be funny but not divorced from credibility."

Hsiao Ch'ang-hua began his theatrical training at the age of eleven and joined his first professional troupe when he was twenty. During his

---

as the result of illness or just sheer overstrain of the vocal chords in constant performance. As in the case of Wang Yao-ch'ing named here, several promising careers were cut short in this way.

3. *Wu-t'ai sheng-huo ssu-shih nien* [Forty years on the stage] 2 (Shanghai, 1953): 14-20.

long life he saw many changes in Chinese society; he ran the gamut of theatrical experience and there were few who could recall with such wealth of detail the hard life of the theater in Imperial China. Old Hsiao was an instructor in the famous Hsi Lien Ch'eng, later the Fu Lien Ch'eng,[4] training school in Peking, from the time it opened its doors at the beginning of the century to its closing in the forties. Teachers in the old training schools were always professionals, and during the forty years of the school's existence some of China's most famous actors passed through Hsiao's hands. There was little he did not know about actors and acting, although it was as the first among clowns, *ch'ou chung-ti i-jen,* that he will go down in the records of the last most important phase of the Peking theater.

A brief synopsis of the plot of this play may next be timely. Su-san, a young courtesan[5] of great charm and popularity has been falsely accused of the murder of a wealthy merchant who had trapped her into becoming his concubine. Previous to this she had been involved in a passionate love affair with a profligate young scholar. Having squandered all his patrimony

4. This was the most celebrated Peking training school during the present century. It was compelled to close down when war began with Japan. Many of China's most illustrious actors had been pupils at the school where traditionally no girls were admitted. Each graduating class of students in the school was identified by a coded system in which the student adopted the second character of his professional name (always different from his given name) from a series of seven code characters indicating the seven classes which graduated from the school during its forty years of activity. The code characters were *hsi, lien, fu, sheng, shih, yüan, yün.* For example, the famous *sheng* actor Ma Lien-lang was a student, the second character of his name indicating that he passed out in the second class.

5. The singsong girls formed a considerable cross section of urban life in traditional China, and were an accepted feature of a social system which recognized double standards by sanctioning concubinage. These women had their own hierarchies ranging from the celebrated courtesans who were talented artists, mixing only with a scholarly governing elite while living in sensual luxury of the most refined kind, down to the simple prostitute with scant pretension to intellectual accomplishments. As with the geisha in Japan, no convivial occasion was complete without the presence of singsong girls long celebrated in literature and the theater. But whatever their status in demimondaine society, they were bound by contract to the houses where they held court or the restaurants and taverns where they plied their professional skills and physical charms. A majority of them came from humble circumstances, and as this play indicates, poor parents sometimes sold their daughters into a life in the pleasure quarters as a last desperate resort, particularly in times of famine. Practically the only way of their regaining freedom was if some well-to-do admirer could provide the vast sums required as ransom to buy a favorite out of bondage and take her as a legal concubine.

on his pretty mistress, he was turned out of the pleasure quarters as being a "squeezed orange." Penniless and destitute, he took refuge in a temple, where he was eventually sought out by his courtesan sweetheart who provided him with money to go and sit for the imperial examinations[6] at Nanking, a panacea for so many lovers' problems on the Chinese stage and an unfailing source of inspiration for the playwrights. After the downfall of her lover, Su-san was pursued by a wealthy merchant whose advances she rejected; the merchant thereupon arranged a clandestine deal to buy her out of bondage in the pleasure quarters and make her his concubine. In furtherance of his designs he lured the girl to his hometown with a faked message from her lover. The jealous wife of the merchant tried to kill Su-san by poisoning food which was eaten in error by her husband, who died instantaneously. The merchant's wife then accused Su-san of the deed and with the help of accomplices she bribed the local magistrate, a recurring villain of the piece on the Chinese stage, into extorting a false confession from Su-san and sentencing her to death.

Under the old Chinese judicial system, once a prisoner had been sentenced to death by the local authority it was mandatory to send the case for retrial at the provincial assizes. After being tried and sentenced locally, therefore, Su-san was sent to T'ai-yüan, the provincial capital of Shansi,

---

6. Imperial examinations: The scholar-official caste which governed China for more than a thousand years was recruited by means of a hallowed system of literary examinations which was discontinued in 1905. In principle, the examinations were open to the humblest in the land who could prove their talent. In point of fact, certain classes of people were forbidden to sit for the examinations because of their "mean" occupations and this included all actors whatever their fame. This did not prevent their playing the part on stage, and the theme of the young hero who sets out for the capital to win honor and justify true love as a successful examination candidate, is one whose implications underlie many a theatrical plot. *A Girl Setting Out for Trial* is a good case in point.

The way to final success in the examinations was long and arduous and the system was organized at three levels. The first hurdle was a district examination in which the successful candidate became a *hsiu-ts'ai* or "budding talent." The second and more difficult test was the provincial examination held triennially in the autumn, followed by the prestigious metropolitan examination held in the Imperial capital in the following spring. Successful candidates in the provincial examinations became *chü-jen*, "promoted men" while those who survived the metropolitan examination became *chin-shih*, "scholars of achievement." A final test taken only by the most talented of the metropolitan candidates took place in the Imperial palace itself and the lucky ones here were admitted to the Han Lin Academy, a special body under control of the central government in the capital and a name to inspire both awe and envy in the minds of the thousands of candidates who flocked to the examinations.

for retrial. In accordance with custom, she traveled under escort and hidden on her person she carried a written plea with which she hoped to convince the judges of her innocence. At the T'ai-yüan court, Su-san was brought before the bench presided over by Circuit Judge Wang Chin-lung, her "dear San-lang," now in high office and supported by two provincial officials, Judge Liu and Treasurer Chou. Su-san's plea was discovered, as prearranged, and handed to Circuit Judge Wang. Judge Liu suspected his superior's past relations with the prisoner and set about trying to embarrass him. After pointed questioning of Su-san the situation became clear to everyone. Wang Chin-lung was so distressed by Liu's insinuations that he had to leave the court, and the trial was adjourned. Wang Ching-lung was able to have a brief meeting with Su-san and arranged to visit her in the cells that night. He was surprised in the act by Judge Liu, who immediately called for Wang's dismissal from his post. The more tolerant persuasion of Treasurer Chou prevailed, however, and the trial finally took place. Su-san was found innocent of any crime and her detractors were brought to justice. The happy lovers were again united and married in the presence of the full court.

This melodramatic and involved plot in the best tradition of the market place storyteller, formed the basis for the play *Jade Pavilion of Happiness*. The scene of Su-san setting out for retrial, with which we are immediately concerned, contains three episodes: the arrival of the old warder to conduct his charge on her official journey, their leaving the local jail together, and finally their travelling along the highway to the provincial assizes. On the way the old warder takes pity on the prisoner and tries to make her unpleasant journey as easy as possible. Nearing their destination Su-san confides the story of the concealed plea to her escort and asks for advice as to how best draw the judges' attention to it. The old warder suggests that she should conceal the paper in the mechanism of her fetters so that when she is freed from them in court the plea will drop out and be seen immediately.

It is perhaps better for the logical Western mind not to worry too closely about the consistency of Su-san's references to her lover-judge in the play, for consistency has not always been the strongest point in dramatic pieces which have evolved in the fashion of this one.

The three episodes described are portrayed by means of a stage bare of any scenery or device, the movements and postures of the actors alone being responsible for suggesting the action in relation to changes of environment. The journey along the highway is indicated by a continuous slow circling of the stage area, with pauses for the various interpolations by the comic actor and for dialogue between the two characters. Different rhythm combinations within the meter set the pacing and mood of the action as a whole. There is no very vigorous physical movement in this piece, which tends to be restrained in this aspect. In the case of the comic actor emphasis is given through the nuances of his immediate presence which, at the risk of sounding repetitive, defies the boundaries of written description. The nearest to what might be termed a choreographic climax occurs when, in order to soothe the old warder's ruffled feelings, the more than usually glamorous prisoner massages her escort's wheezy chest.

As she trudges along the hot road, the charm and pathos of his prisoner impels the warder to remove the heavy fetters from her shoulders, in defiance of regulations, and ease her physical discomfort until they get nearer their destination. Su-san is overwhelmed with gratitude and on being told by her benefactor that he is a lonely old man without a son or grandchildren, than which there could be no greater calamity according to the Chinese way of thinking, she offers to become his adopted daughter on the spot, an offer which the stage clown turns into something other than mere filial jubilation. As they continue their journey, Su-san voices her hatred of society through song, climaxing her outpouring of feelings by denouncing every man in Hu-t'ung district for having been so indifferent to her fate. This is too much for the old warder, who takes umbrage at the slur upon his native district and therefore himself by implication. Su-san calms his wrath with soothing words and caresses.

As she circles the stage and throughout the sung narration of her particular personal hatreds, Su-san is interrupted each time by the old warder who, with a combination of shattering cynicism mingled with a generous dash of old roguery, points out the inevitability of events considering the chain of circumstances. The failure of good government through human fallibility, forms the burden of the warder's quips.

Obviously the social values which condoned both a Su-san and her persecutors are outrageous when judged in the hindsight of today's attitudes in China, but if the mockery of the stage clown in this case seems as much a reason for bitter as good-humored laughter, it must also be recognized that this has always been the purgative nature of the clown's attack if not its justification. History offers little proof that we can afford to dispense with his functions.

The skill and finesse demanded of the clown in this play have already been noted; certainly a practiced hand was needed to make this part good theater. Although nurtured upon his immediate world of traditional Chinese society, the old warder's cynical comments on hallowed ethics and vested authority, alternating with his digs about sex and self-interest as he addresses his audience directly, smack of the clown's universality. Issues are evaded, facts are stood on their head, and jibes puncture any pretensions to take things too seriously. In his capacity of twice-removed commentator, the clown here exploits the incongruity of theater to point to the inner contradictions of his public.

Jade Pavilion of Happiness, of which *A Girl Setting Out for Trial* is a part, had a popularity which died hard among audiences in China. It was once described as a play "symptomatic of the sentimental-erotic ideas" of the Chinese.[7] One of the last major performances[8] was announced in the Peking press of August 1962 when special performances were given by combined Peking troupes in commemoration of the actor Mei Lanfang, deceased the previous year who, in collaboration with the comic actor Hsiao Ch'ang-hua, brought such luster to the play in times past.

Musically this piece typifies the time-honored Asian tradition of letting ready-made metrical patterns serve the functions of evoking mood and stimulating psychological involvement. The music is completely interrelated with the stage action, advancing the interwoven patterns of both gestural and vocal movement as well as underscoring dramatic intensity, in this case resulting from the feeling of anguish implicit through the prisoner's plight.

A Girl Setting Out for Trial is categorized as a *p'i-huang* play, a portmanteau word derived from *hsi-p'i* and *erh-huang,* the names of two musical styles which developed in different regional areas and were influenced again by other regional forms in their gradual evolution and final acceptance as the principal form of musical expression used in the Peking-style theater. It is indicative of the composite nature in general of an entertainment whose stage techniques were perfected during a long process of assimilation from many other theatrical sources.

The instruments used on the Peking stage have been described in some

---

7. By the English writer Harold Acton.

8. A scene from *Jade Pavilion of Happiness* was also performed by the Peking Visiting Troupe to Hongkong in 1963. Their tour was one of the highlights of the Chinese entertainment world in Hongkong at the time. The troupe was led by the actors Ma Lien-lang and Chang Chü-ch'iu, old favorites of the fans in that city.

detail in the first volume of this series. Briefly, they consist of stringed instruments and percussion as the principal means of accompaniment, with some wind instruments serving as accessories and occasionally, as in the case of the flute, taking the lead. The backbone of the Peking-stage instrumental ensemble, however, consists of a bowed, two-stringed instrument called the *hu-ch'in* and a secondary plucked string instrument, *yüeh-ch'in*, a hardwood drum with a skin head beaten with two thin sticks, and a pair of redwood clappers held in the drummer's left hand and used to beat out the metrical stress rather in the manner of castanets. The percussion section of the orchestra includes a large and small gong plus cymbals, which are all used to mark exits and entries, to time movement and gesture, and to accentuate emotional climaxes in the action of the play and song. It will be noticed from the translated text of the play that there is a standardized repertoire of percussive metrical patterns for use in stipulated situations just as there are of the string music which accompanies the actors' singing.

The two main categories of *erh-huang* and *hsi-p'i* music might be described as fountainheads, providing a prescribed number of metrical arrangements which are used over and over again in varying sequence to suit a particular dramatic situation and whose names immediately convey to the Chinese musician the particular metrical arrangement they embody. The distinction between these two principal categories lies in the different tunings required on the *hu-ch'in*'s double strings. In the past, musical meter has always been defined by the Chinese in terms of *pan,* the stressed beat, and *yen,* the unstressed beat, in a measure. For example, a great part of the time Su-san pours out her troubles on the stage, she is described as singing in *hsi-p'i-yuan-pan.* The first two words, of course, indicate the main musical category as named above while the last two words indicate a standard, or primary, beat. A theater musician, hearing this term, would instantly know that it stands for a metrical combination designated as *i-pan, i-yen,* indicating a metrical signature comparable to the Western $\frac{2}{4}$ time, that is to say, with the rhythmic pattern of the measure defined within a total of two quarter notes and approximating to *andante,* literally a movement that is neither running nor standing still, but going along in moderate fashion. The Chinese theater musician knows the repertoire by heart and requires no printed notation. He reacts instinctively to the particular rhythmic combination that relates to the specific dramatic-musical occasion.

At the beginning of the play Su-san pleads with "Heaven above" in a

despairing song which is described as being in *fan erh-huang man-pan.*
The last two words indicate a metrical pattern of *i-pan, san-yen,* or one
stressed, three unstressed beats to the measure, a slow rhythm. The word
fan literally means "turning back" and is a qualifying term indicating a
degree of mood and intensity in the singing style which is comparable
to the Western *con dolore,* "with grief." *Fan erh-huang* requires a special
tuning of the strings which differs from that of the main *erh-huang* category. The lingering melancholy effect characteristic of the vocal quality
in this case is one that essentially expresses despair and sorrow. The
rhythmic combination upon which it is based is used to induce such a
mood not only in this play but many others where a situation demands
it.

The word *man* literally means "slow," which is self-explanatory, although as in Western music the rhythmic combination within the measure can vary with an identical time signature. For example, the two
main categories of Peking-stage music have a *man* or slow timing designated respectively as *hsi-p'i man-pan* and *erh-huang man-pan.* Both terms
designate a time signature comparable to $\frac{4}{4}$ time, but they each arrive at
this timing by using completely different metrical combinations within
the measure. In conjunction with such principles, the pitch and enunciation of the actor's voice, both in the sung and spoken word, must be
considered in relation to the metrical combinations employed in the
string and percussive accompaniment.

Whether dialogue is in verse or prose, it invariably embodies a musical
element which identifies song and speech with the rhythmic flow of the
actor's gestures. Methods of breathing emphasize use of the open mouth
for gutteral sounds, restricted enunciation for the "sharp" sounds, and a
space left between the tongue and the palate for the palatal sounds. Certain words in the *erh-huang* and *hsi-p'i* patterns must be given different
pronunciation from the Peking way, particularly in the sharp sounds
which must be relaxed or contracted in a greater degree. Yet again there
are a number of words in the theatrical idiom which require pronouncing
in Hupeh dialect style with the point of the tongue against the teeth,
what are known as *shang k'ou-tzu,* "liquid" words.

These are general rules pertaining to all actors with the exception of
those who play the comic roles and are therefore far less restricted by
formal rules of enunciation.

Description such as this can obviously do little more than give some
idea of the meaning of certain general principles and their technical func-

tion not only in *Jade Pavilion of Happiness* but all Peking-style plays. Their animation is dependent on a highly individual musical style, which no Western idiom can satisfactorily replace without destroying the inner structure of stage performance.

A Girl Setting Out for Trial

Scene 1

The stage is devoid of anything at all. There is a curtain as backdrop with an entry right stage, i.e., left of the audience, and an exit left stage, i.e., right of the audience. The voice of the old warder Ch'ung Kung-tao is heard offstage.

CH'UNG KUNG-TAO: Ah ho!
> *(This is followed by a percussive passage beaten out by the drum, gongs, and cymbals of the orchestra to accompany the actor's entry. The percussion players draw upon an extensive repertoire of rhythmic arrangements, each known by a special name, used for entries, exits, timing of movement, emphasis of mood during the singing and stage action, and so on. The name of this particular arrangement, one often used for the actor's entry, is wu chi-t'ou and its onomatopoeic pattern in Chinese would read: ta, tai, ch'iang, ts'ai ch'iang, ts'ai, ch'iang. Ta represents the drum beat, tai the small gong, ch'iang the combined beat of large and small gongs and the cymbals in forceful emphasis, while ts'ai represents the small gong beaten together with the cymbals, the accent being taken on the three ch'iangs. The old warder enters right stage shaking his uplifted right forefinger and moving to down center stage, i.e., to the front center of the stage facing the audience. His body is inclined a little forward from the waist; he walks with legs bent at the knees and his feet turned outwards a little. His steps are short, and his shoulders move in time to the swing of his waist as the weight is taken on the heel before each foot is placed squarely on the ground. The movements of both the actors in this play are restrained rather than spectacular and tend to be limited by the*

*nature of the play. In the first place, both characters are restricted
to circling the stage at a slow and measured pace timed to the
rhythm of the singing, and for part of this time Su-san's hands are
manacled. In her case, choreographic variation is only introduced
when she is freed from her chains for a time, and then consists
largely of the graceful hand gestures used by the performer of
women's roles to reinforce song and dialogue and accentuate
posturing. It is the comic actor's function to provide the counter-
balance to Su-san's role which is largely a singing one. It would be
idle to describe the old warder's technique in terms of structured
gesture and movement, although of course these are ever present
in his performance. A knowing look, a devastating aside, the facial
expression that only the clown is capable of under his white make-
up evade the restrictive nature of written description. Like all
comic roles, this one calls for a masterly sense of timing, improvisation, a ready wit, all those indispensable qualities in fact, which
bring alive the comic art in demanding that sheer gusto of presence
that is the dividing line between the run of the mill performer and
the talented clown.)*

CH'UNG KUNG-TAO:

You say you are right,
I say I am right.
Who is right or not
Only Heaven knows.[9]
(*He stands to face the audience from the front of the stage, indicat-
ing his person by pointing inwards towards his chest, a gesture that
was only used by the comic actor. He is still in the same stance,
knees bent, feet apart and turned outwards slightly.*)
As for me,
Ch'ung Kung-tao
Of Hung-t'ung district,
I'm a warder in charge of prisoner escort.

---

9. *Ni shuo ni kung tao,
Wo shuo wo kung tao,
Kung tao pu kung tao,
Tzu yu t'ien chih tao.*
When the wine cups were being replenished at many an after-the-theater supper
in the past, there was no quotation that sprang more readily to the lips of a theater
fan than the old warder's opening speech.

Today an official dispatch arrived from the Prefect
Ordering Su-san to travel under arrest
And set out for trial.
Depart and travel,
Travel and depart.[10]
I mention it since I'm here as a go-between.
(*He turns and goes toward the rear curtain and stops to call out in a rolling Peking burr.*)
Is there anyone there?
(*A jailer ambles out, the part being played in raucous hsiao-ch'ou fashion.*)

JAILER: What's up with you?

CH'UNG KUNG-TAO: I'm the commander-in-chief of prisoner escorts.

JAILER (*sarcastically*):
Your honour!

CH'UNG KUNG-TAO: Shut up.
Might you have someone called Su-san in jail?

JAILER: I have.

CH'UNG KUNG-TAO: Bring her out. We've got to get going.

JAILER (*bawling*):
Su-san, get a move on!
(*He exits. Su-san's voice is heard off stage in a long, lingering wail which drops into silence. Literally it means "Oh how bitter," but technically it is treated as pure sound pattern and is almost onomatopoeic in effect:*)

SU-SAN'S VOICE: K'u wa!
(*The percussion section of the orchestra brings Su-san on stage with a passage known as niu-ssu. The drum is beaten with both sticks twice emphatically and then with a light rapid tattoo leading into an arrangement which runs tai, ch'iang, tai, ts'ai, tai, i, tai, ch'iang, tai, ts'ai, ch'iang, tai, ts'ai, tai, tai, ch'iang. The sound symbolism of these is the same as before. Su-san now enters and utters a shrill, descending cry of despair:*)

SU-SAN: Wei-ya!
(*The niu-ssu passage is taken by the percussion again and Su-san*)

---

10. *Hsing, hsing, ch'ü, ch'ü;*
   Ch'ü, ch'ü, hsing, hsing.
Alliteration of a kind common in the comic actor's monologues.

prepares to sing in erh-huang yao-pan as the hu-ch'in begins to play.)
Suddenly I hear the name Su-san called.
My spirit fails me and I am filled with terror.
I dare not go forward; but I have no choice,
I must drag myself on.
I will ask that old fellow the reason for my summons.
(*She relapses into the shrill and highly formalized speech of the women's roles.*)
Venerable sir, I am here.

CH'UNG KUNG-TAO: You are Su-san?

SU-SAN: Indeed that is my name.

CH'UNG KUNG-TAO: Ah, Su-san, congratulations!
(*He uses the expression ta hsi, a conventional term meaning congratulations, but it was also used in an inversely polite sense to indicate commiseration with a condemned person.*)

SU-SAN: Ah, venerable sir, I have been deeply wronged.
Why is it a matter for congratulations?

CH'UNG KUNG-TAO: You're going to be taken for trial.

SU-SAN (*startled*): What, I am being taken for trial?

CH'UNG KUNG-TAO: That's right.

SU-SAN: But where?

CH'UNG KUNG-TAO: To the Prefectural Court.

SU-SAN: But who is going to take me such a distance?

CH'UNG KUNG-TAO: Why, poor old me of course, Ch'ung Kung-tao.

SU-SAN: When do we start on the journey?

CH'UNG KUNG-TAO: Tell me when you're ready to go and we'll go.

SU-SAN: Venerable sir, go and get your baggage while I pay my farewell respects to the god of the jail; then I shall be ready to hurry on the way.

CH'UNG KUNG-TAO: Right, I'll go and put a few things together while you get ready; then I'll be right back.
(*He exits up right. There is a percussion passage from the orchestra, ta-lo i-chi lo, onomatopoeically represented as cha cha ch'iang, cha representing the beat of the redwood clappers and ch'iang, the combined beat of large gong, small gong and cymbals preceding Su-san's spoken words.*)

SU-SAN: Ah, Heaven above! Know that I, Su-san, suffer a great injustice.
How can I make someone understand?
(*There is another percussive passage ta-lo chu-t'ou, rendered as ta,*

tai, ch'iang, ts'ai, tai, ch'iang, i.e., drum, small gong, combined percussion, small gong and cymbals, small gong, combined percussion.)

SU-SAN (*begins to sing in fan erh-huang man-pan*):

That old man Ch'ung says it is a wrong that will be difficult to put right. I recall Wang Chin-lung, a young gentleman forgetful of past kindness. I remember the first time we met. We were fond of each other, so his integrity will remain firm as a rock when he meets me face to face. I kneel down here in supplication first. I shall respectfully plead my cause and the gods will listen carefully to this slave's words. They will protect me when I meet San Lang. If my life is spared I will restore a temple with painted gold leaf.

(*Ch'ung Kung-tao enters up right carrying the fish-shaped cangue*[11] *folded in two under his arm.*)

CH'UNG KUNG-TAO (*rolling out his words in Peking style*):

Have you finished your farewells?

SU-SAN: I am ready.

CH'UNG KUNG-TAO (*stepping towards her with the cangue*):

Then put on the cangue.

SU-SAN: Must I really wear the cangue?

CH'UNG KUNG-TAO (*brusquely*):

It's the law of the land as decreed by the Emperor. You must put it on.

SU-SAN (*wailing*):

Wei-ya!

---

11. The cangue, *chia* in Chinese, was a heavy wooden square collar made in two sections with holes for the head and hands through which the prisoner was locked in, the whole contraption resting on the shoulders of the wearer. To put on the cangue and be manacled, *p'ei chia tai so,* was how the Chinese described the punishment. Authorities believe the word cangue was derived from the Portuguese word *canga,* meaning a yoke, which is certainly descriptive. Prisoners sentenced to wear the cangue were confined to it during the day but were allowed to take it off at night. All criminals were compelled to wear it when being led through the streets as is made clear by Ch'ung Kung-tao in the play.

The stage-property cangue worn by Su-san was a far more decorative affair than its real-life prototype. It was made from light chromium polished metal, and the two halves were constructed in the form of a fish, a carp. The Chinese called the carp the "messenger fish" after an old legend about a man who discovered a letter inside the belly of a carp, hence the significance. It is a good example of the kind of symbolism within symbolism often found in the decoration and the motifs of costumes and properties on the Peking stage.

(She kneels down to have the cangue fitted over her head and shoulders. The two pieces of bright metal shaped like the halves of a carp are fitted round her neck, the opening for this being in the head of the fish; the raised clenched fists are manacled with a chain round the wrists and placed through two holes in the tail end of the fish. Clamps on the two halves hold the whole contraption together in one piece, the effect being that Su-san's manacled hands are kept raised before her at face level. Although the stage cangue is made of very light metal, it requires considerable skill to sing and converse in this position and the role is one that certainly makes heavy demands on the actor.

SU-SAN *(rising)*:

Ah, venerable sir, I will wait for you at the gate-house while you go and deliver your dispatch.

CH'UNG KUNG-TAO *(artfully)*:

You're an expert at the business all right!

(They separate and exit, Su-san up right, i.e., left of the audience, and the old warder up left, i.e., right of the audience.)

Scene 2

A prison official enters up left calling the roll. Ch'ung Kung-tao enters up right.

PRISON OFFICIAL: Warder in charge of prisoner escort, Ch'ung Kung-tao?

CH'UNG KUNG-TAO: Present!

PRISON OFFICIAL: Assistant Warder Tiger Li?

CH'UNG KUNG-TAO: Present!

PRISON OFFICIAL: How comes one man to be doing two men's duties?

CH'UNG KUNG-TAO: We've gone into partnership and fixed up a deal.

I'm his stand-in. See you later!

(He is about to depart.)

PRISON OFFICIAL: Come back!

CH'UNG KUNG-TAO: What for?

PRISON OFFICIAL *(artfully)*:

Where are you two going?

CH'UNG KUNG-TAO: T'ai-yüan prefecture.

PRISON OFFICIAL: What proof is there of that?

CH'UNG KUNG-TAO: An official dispatch.

PRISON OFFICIAL: Where is it?

CH'UNG KUNG-TAO: It's still on Circuit Judge Wang's desk. See you
    later!

(*He is about to depart.*)

PRISON OFFICIAL: Come back!

CH'UNG KUNG-TAO: What's up?

PRISON OFFICIAL: When you return I want you to bring me back a mule.
    (*The mule was a pack animal much used in Shansi, the setting of
    the play.*)

CH'UNG KUNG-TAO: Weigh out your silver.[12]

PRISON OFFICIAL: Here are twenty-four copper cash.

CH'UNG KUNG-TAO (*scornfully*):
    Twenty-four copper cash? That'll only buy a mule's tail. Nothing
    doing!
    (*What follows is a play on words and meanings which is lost in
    translation, but this cross talk situation is typical of Chinese
    clowning.*)

PRISON OFFICIAL: I don't mean a mule to ride.

CH'UNG KUNG-TAO: What do you mean then?

PRISON OFFICIAL: A horse-hair sieve.

CH'UNG KUNG-TAO: What do you want that for?

PRISON OFFICIAL: To strain the pine resin.

CH'UNG KUNG-TAO: To do what?

PRISON OFFICIAL: Waterproof the paper lantern.

CH'UNG KUNG-TAO: You've got it wrong, pine resin's not for water-
    proofing the lantern.

PRISON OFFICIAL: What's it for?

CH'UNG KUNG-TAO: . . .

PRISON OFFICIAL: You've got it wrong now.

CH'UNG KUNG-TAO: . . .[13]

(*They exit, the prison official up left, Ch'ung Kung-tao up right.*)

12. The Chinese *liang*, or "ounce" of silver, also known as *tael*, was a standard
unit of currency and the equivalent of one thousand copper cash, the only coin
made formerly in China. Silver was made in the shape of small ingots which were
used for payments and could vary in weight from one to one hundred ounces. Different degrees of fineness in the silver used determined the standards of values and
these were by no means consistent throughout the country.

13. The final sally between Ch'ung Kung-tao and the prison official is untrans-
latable, being nonsense dependent on the juxtaposition of words with the same
sound. The Chinese playgoer's ear was readily attuned to what could be called

Scene 3

*Preceding the next entry and signifying an emotion-charged situation
is a percussive passage called k'uai ch'ang ch'ui; it is represented by ta,
ta, ta, ta, yi, yi, kang, kang, kang, ts'ai, tai, ts'ai, kang, ts'ai, tai, ts'ai, ts'ai,
kang, i, ts'ai. Two new syllables occur here: yi, representing the beat of
the wooden clappers, and kang, meaning the large gong beaten alone.
After this passage Su-san enters up right, i.e., left of the audience; she is
of course wearing the cangue and accompanied by the old warder who
now supports himself on a wooden stave for the journey.*

SU-SAN: Ai-ya!
> (*She begins to sing in liu-shui pan as the hu-ch'in leads in.*)
> Leaving Hung-t'ung district,
> I am led along the wide streets.
> I have not begun to speak the sorrow in my heart.
> You passing gentlemen, listen to this slave's words.
> Whoever is going to Nanking,
> Please take my dear San-lang a letter.
> Say that Su-san brings a case to judgment.
> Though I become a horse or a dog in the next world,
> I'll repay you for your kindness.
> (*She kneels down in supplication.*)
CH'UNG KUNG-TAO (*bringing things down to earth*):
> Why are you kneeling down there? Are you invoking heaven and
> earth or just begging for traveling expenses?
SU-SAN: I am neither invoking heaven and earth nor begging for travel-
> ing expenses. I implore you, sir, to enquire at the next inn if there
> is anyone going to Nanking.
CH'UNG KUNG-TAO: Why do you want to know if there's anyone going
> to Nanking?
SU-SAN: To take my dear San-lang a letter.
CH'UNG KUNG-TAO: Right, well here we are.
> (*Addressing the audience.*)

---

punning with sound, a common practice arising from the nature of the language.
The Chinese reads as follows in romanization:
> Ch'ung Kung-tao: Shih huang-la
> Prison official: Ni yeh ts'o la shih lung-huang
> Ch'ung Kung-tao: Cha, cha, cha, shih lung-huang

She's still anxious about her sweetheart. Gentlemen, how would you like to know a girl like this? Put down a couple of copper coins and you may get change for a hundred ounces of silver. (*To Su-san.*) I'll just go and find out for you.

CH'UNG KUNG-TAO (*turns towards the backdrop curtain and, moving close to it, calls out*):

I say there!

TRAVELER'S VOICE (*behind curtain*):

Well?

CH'UNG KUNG-TAO: Is there anyone there bound for Nanking?

TRAVELER'S VOICE: A party went off three days ago.

CH'UNG KUNG-TAO: And today?

TRAVELER'S VOICE: There's only someone going to the Lapa[14] Temple at Kalgan[15] with a train of camels.

(*The camel was an important pack animal used by traders in North China.*)

CH'UNG KUNG-TAO: Aiya! (*Turning to Su-san.*) Su-san, we're out of luck. A party went off to Nanking three days ago, but now there's only someone going to the Lapa Temple at Kalgan with a train of camels.

SU-SAN (*weeps*):

Ah!

(*It is a long drawn-out wail preceded by a rapid tattoo on the drum*

---

14. La-pa: A slender brass trumpet about three and a half feet long and having a shrill note. It was used by drivers of camel caravans as a signal when leading their teams in and out of Peking. This fact underlies the allusion in the play where the word *la-pa* is also turned into a pun on *lama*, meaning a Tibetan Buddhist priest, and is again indicative of the kind of word play which amused the ordinary Chinese audience in the past. At one time this instrument was used in the Peking theater orchestra, where it served to sound the conclusion of the play, among other functions. In stage circles there was an expression *ch'ui-t'ai*, literally "blow the stage," meaning to announce the end of the performance. This expression became current in everyday speech to mean "that's the end of that." Yet another colloquialism was *ch'ui la-pa* with exactly the same meaning as the English "blowing his own trumpet."

15. When Su-san pleaded for a messenger going to Nanking there could have been no more frustrating response than the one she received. Kalgan was a trading town for Mongolia situated to the far Northwest of Peking on the outskirts of the Great Wall, Nanking, the imperial capital from A.D. 1356-1421, the period of the play's action, lay to the far south in Kiangsu province. The two towns then were so remote from each other as to make Su-san's request irrelevant.

with both sticks and followed by tai, ch'iang, a beat on the small
gong and then the gongs and cymbals in unison.)
I am destined to misfortune!
CH'UNG KUNG-TAO: Let's move on.
(*The hu-ch'in begins to play, and Su-san commences to sing in*
hsi-p'i k'uai-pan.)
SU-SAN: People say Loyang[16] flowers are like delicate embroidery.[17]
But confined to prison,
How can one know the spring?
I bow my head crossing the boundaries of Hung-t'ung district.
(*During this song they have begun their slow perambulation round*
the stage. The old warder comes to a stop at the conclusion of
Su-san's song.)
Sir, for what reason have you halted?
CH'UNG KUNG-TAO (*turning towards her*):
It's such a hot day and, although I have this staff to help me along,
I'm still fagged out; but you have to endure it with that heavy
cangue on your shoulders. Wait until I help you off with it.
SU-SAN (*surprised*):
But does the law decreed by the Imperial Court permit me to
travel in such a way?
CH'UNG KUNG-TAO: Out here I represent the law of the land! Now we
are clear of the city you may rely on me. Come, let me help you
off with it.
(*Su-san kneels before him and he removes the cangue, which from*
now on he carries under his arm, folded in two halves.)
SU-SAN: I'm giving you a lot of trouble, sir.
(*Rising.*)
You are indeed a very kind person.
CH'UNG KUNG-TAO: Kind person maybe, and yet I have no son to
succeed me.

16. Loyang was the capital of the eastern Han dynasty, A.D. 25-220, and later
of the Wei kingdom, A.D. 220-265. It was situated in present day Honan province,
and its glories as a cultural, religious, and political center have gone down in
history. As in other ancient cities, the beauty and the talents of the singing girls
and courtesans who were a part of the social scene created a literary legend.
17. The term *hua ju chin*, "flowers like embroidery," was a poetic way of
expressing the elegant beauty of blossoms and in this case the courtesans of
Loyang, *hua*, flower, being a common euphemism in Chinese for the demimondaine
and her environment.

SU-SAN: Aiya! So kind a person and yet to have no son at all!

CH'UNG KUNG-TAO: Well, not to have a son[18] is one thing, but not to have grandchildren is even worse!

SU-SAN: You may laugh at me, sir, but if you do not scorn the idea, I am willing to take your name and become your adopted daughter.

CH'UNG KUNG-TAO: Say no more! That I should get such a lucky chance as this!

SU-SAN (*kneeling down before him*):
Father, I pay my respects. Your daughter salutes you.

CH'UNG KUNG-TAO: Stand up, stand up!

(*He bursts into a crescendo of laughter.*)

Ho, ho, ho, ho, ei, ya, ya. I never thought that today I should get such a fine adopted daughter, such a godchild. I can live on her now and fling my money around, wear a fur coat, have a good time, drive about in a motorcar, and play mahjong. I've certainly struck a good thing. And if anybody asks, "Who's that old boy?" I'll just say it's so and so's adopted father.

(*The name of the leading actor playing Su-san was customarily inserted at this point.*)

Ho, ho, ho!

(*Changing his mood.*)

Aiya! But this poor old adopted father has no gift to offer for the occasion. Very well, here's an idea! I'll make you a present of this staff to help you along. Then you can call yourself by a new name—Three Legs!

18. In traditional China a man without children was a subject for commiseration, and for a man to have no son was a personal tragedy. In Confucian society the institution of marriage was built around the continuance of the patrilineal family line, and a man who failed in this matter was regarded as lacking in his obligations to society, while a woman who did not produce a son failed in her obligations to matrimony. Double standards prevailed as a result, and concubinage was sanctioned as a means of ensuring male descendants. A second way was through adoption, which became an accepted social practice in China, where a man might adopt an heir from within his own family on his father's side or from acceptable circles outside the family. The last was particularly true in the case of crafts, trades, and professions, where a man would not only want his family name perpetuated but his personal skills. An actor, for example, often took an adopted "son" if there were none to carry on the tradition of their art. Adoption laid strict obligations on both parties to preserve the canons of family relationships, although obviously the system laid itself open to abuses as well as advantages. The adoption of a "daughter," and a courtesan at that, must be treated in the light of theatrical expediency and romantic association rather than anything else.

(This is a reference to a Chinese proverb san chiao ha-ma, the three-legged toad, a rarity found only on the moon according to legend.)
SU-SAN: Thank you indeed, father.
Shall we go on?
(They continue their promenade as the hu-ch'in plays, and Su-san sings a short passage in hsi-p'i tao-pan. Even a melodramatic sentence like this becomes an elongated pattern of musical sound in which the literal meaning of the words is aurally sacrificed to metrical stress, rhyme, and elision, and this applies to most stage singing. The role of Su-san is, or was, considered a musical tour-de-force of its kind. The comic role, in contrast, has no sung lines in this play.)
Have compassion on the former courtesan whose tears rain down.
(There is a percussive passage man ch'ang ch'ui rendered as ta, ta, yi, yi, kang, tz'u, tai, tz'u, kang, tz'u, tai, tz'u, kang, tz'u, tai, tz'u, tai, tai, tai, tai, kang, ts'ai i, kang, ta, tz'u, tai, kang, and Su-san begins to sing in hsi-p'i man-pan.)
I grieve when I recall the past.
In those days I was elegantly dressed,
Where now I wear a prisoner's clothes.
CH'UNG KUNG-TAO *(halting)*:
All right, my child, you tell us when you began life as a courtesan you were elegantly dressed, but now you have sunk to wearing prison clothes. So, to begin with, you were dressed like somebody, but on the stage you are dressed like nobody.[19] All the same I reckon you are still somebody. Let's go on.
(The hu-ch'in plays, and Su-san begins to sing in hsi-p'i yüan-pan as they recommence their promenade.)

---

19. In the Chinese original Ch'ung Kung-tao makes his comparison by means of the two terms *ta hung-jen,* literally "important person in red," and *ta hung i-fu,* literally "deep red clothing." Red was the color of the ornamental "button" fixed on the crown of the hat of an *i-p'in kuan,* or official of the first rank in the old Chinese civil service. The term *ta hung-jen,* therefore, passed into usage as indicating someone with social standing, "a big noise" or a "big shot" to use our contemporary English slang. Red was also the color used for women's prison clothing, and Su-san's stage costume in this play consists of a scarlet silk tunic and trousers to symbolize her misfortune, albeit in a theatrically decorative way. The double play on words and symbolism and the clown's pointed reference to *stage* costume, emphasizing the pretence of theater, typify dialogue methods used on the Peking stage and at the same time indicate how nuances must often be sacrificed when trying to render the Chinese clown's patter in English.

SU-SAN: I hate my cruel-hearted parents for their avarice in selling me
     into slavery as a courtesan.
CH'UNG KUNG-TAO (*halting to say his piece*):
     Your parents had a reason for selling their own daughter in that
     way. They didn't do it willingly, I'm certain. They were destitute
     and it was their last resort. But that's all past. No use bearing a
     grudge against them now. If you come to think of it, you might
     have been much worse off as a wild fowl than a caged bird.[20] Let's
     move on.
     (*They recommence their promenade.*)
SU-SAN (*singing in hsi-p'i yüan-pan*):
     I hate Shen Yen-lin, the Shansi merchant.
     What right had he to buy my body?
CH'UNG KUNG-TAO (*halting*):
     Such talk shows you have no conscience. Shen Yen-lin put down
     a pile of money to buy you out and give you your freedom. What's
     wrong about that?
     (*Coughs.*)
     Come to think of it, he wasn't right either. He already had one wife.
     Why did he want to take you home to play with? You can't tether
     two donkeys in the same stable. But you were young and pretty,
     so, being bored with his wife, Shen spent all his time with you
     instead. It's no wonder that a little vinegar[21] found its way into
     the sauce. And in that situation the storm soon blew up, eh?
SU-SAN: Let's go on.
     (*The hu-ch'in plays as they continue their promenade and Su-san
     sings in hsi-p'i yüan-pan.*)
     I hate his wife P'i-shih for her cruelty.
     She ought not to have poisoned her husband.
CH'UNG KUNG-TAO: (*halting progress once again*)
     You say P'i-shih shouldn't have poisoned her husband's food. But
     it's all clear as daylight. You had become his favorite concubine so
     naturally she felt malicious. She poisoned the dish of noodles in

---

20. The expression used here by Ch'ung Kung-tao is *yeh-chi,* a pheasant or wild
fowl, a term which also implies a common prostitute in Chinese. The old warder is
cynically suggesting, therefore, that the life of a pampered high-class courtesan is
preferable to that of a streetwalker.
    21. Vinegar symbolizes jealousy. The Chinese talk about a *ts'u kuan-tzu,* vinegar
jar, meaning a jealous woman. To drink vinegar, *ch'ih ts'u,* means to be jealous.

order to get rid of you. She never dreamed her husband would eat them instead.

(*Addressing the audience.*)

Alas, let this be a warning to you, gentlemen. Hereafter, when you want to buy a concubine you'd better consult your wife first, if you don't want a life of trouble.

SU-SAN: Let us go on.

(*Again the hu-ch'in plays and again Su-san begins to sing in hsi-p'i yüan-pan.*)

I hate Ch'un-chin, that pleasure-loving little minx. She plotted treachery with Chao Chien-sheng.

CH'UNG KUNG-TAO (*halting again*):

Why call Ch'un-chin names? She's only a slave girl employed as a servant by P'i-shih to whom she belongs. You can't expect her to be on your side.

(*Pause.*)

But I must say she's a fast little piece, and don't I know it! She's usually decked out in her powder and paint when I see her. Come sundown, you'll find her standing at the door showing herself off, peeking on every side to attract attention, while ogling all the young men. Not only them. When I was passing her door the other day she gave me such a look my heart missed a beat. But at my time of life (*he grunts*) it's too late for that kind of thing.

Let's go on.

SU-SAN: Let's go on.

(*They recommence their promenade, the hu-ch'in plays, and Su-san sings in hsi-p'i yüan-pan.*)

I hate that corrupt District Magistrate, Wang.

(*Again this short line is of considerable musical duration and takes them round a proportionate distance of stage.*)

CH'UNG KUNG-TAO (*halting*):

So you hate the corrupt District Magistrate, Wang? You really open your mouth without thinking. Don't you know the saying: "To be in an official position requires great ability" and doesn't that mean getting rich? You were just unlucky that your official happened to have too much ability. Say no more.

Let's go on.

(*They move on, the hu-ch'in plays, and Su-san sings in hsi-p'i yüan-pan.*)

SU-SAN: I hate the yamen officials for sharing the bribe.

CH'UNG KUNG-TAO (*halting his progress for a vehement defense of his own class and a sardonic comment on "them" as against "us"*): Su-san, the more you talk the more muddle-headed you sound. In order to hold an official post you must accept bribes. It cannot be avoided. Naturally we underlings must also get our cut. Look at these boots of mine. How do you suppose I got them? I had to buy them, and where do you suppose I got the cash? If you live near the mountains you get your living from the mountains; if you live near the river you get your living from the river. What's the point of hating people like me? If you hate us, why do you go to law?

Let's move on.

(*The inference here is big fleas have little fleas. High satin boots were an item in the official uniform supposedly issued to petty ranking members of the civil service, but even the outer trappings of rank had their price. This is a comment on public acceptance of official corruption by the end of the nineteenth century when this play became structured in its present form. They move on and Su-san sings in hsi-p'i yüan-pan.*)

SU-SAN: I hate the magistrate's assistants for agreeing to torture me.

(*They halt once more.*)

CH'UNG KUNG-TAO: Su-san, you don't understand. When an official has accepted a bribe, he's uncertain what to do if a prisoner refuses to confess. He becomes worried. There's no way out for him, he has to use torture and his assistants must go along with his decision. What else do you hate?

Let's go. Let's go.

(*They continue their promenade and Su-san sings in hsi-p'i yüan-pan.*)

SU-SAN: I hate and detest Li-hu, the torturer, who made me confess.

CH'UNG KUNG-TAO (*halting*): Li-hu was bribed by P'i-shih to make you confess. Think what you are saying, control your speech, child. You should blame it on your fate for having got you into this criminal affair. Say no more. Hurry along.

(*They recommence their promenade. The mood is one of quickened agitation, and Su-san changes to liu-shui pan.*)

SU-SAN: Ai!

The more I think of it the more hateful it all becomes. There is not a single good man in all Hung-t'ung district!

CH'UNG KUNG-TAO (*is deeply affronted by this slur on his native district and therefore himself and he challenges Su-san sharply.*)
What? So there's not a single good man in all Hung-t'ung district? What a thing to say! So, I'm no good eh? So that's how you take advantage of me? Let's put an end to it ... before I get angry ... Really ...

SU-SAN: Ya!
(*She realizes she has gone too far and sets out to soothe the old warder's ruffled feelings. The hu-ch'in begins and she sings in hsi-p'i liu-shui pan.*)
A word hastily spoken has aroused my father's anger. I must regain his favor with kind words.
(*She walks towards him from down left center to down center—i.e., the warder is at a point near the center front of the stage—but he turns away from her.*)
Ah, father, father, ya!
(*There is a percussive passage t'an chien feng tien t'ou indicated by the symbols ta, ta, yi, yi, ch'iang, ts'ai, ch'iang, lai, ts'ai, yi, lai, ch'iang. The new symbol here is lai representing a light beat on the small gong. Su-san changes to hui-lung meter. In a cajoling manner:*)
You are the best person in the world!
(*At this point Su-san is standing directly to the left of the old warder, who faces the audience front. His knees are bent, feet wide apart, and he supports himself on the cangue held directly on the ground in front of him, right hand on top of the left hand placed on the carp's head which is the uppermost portion of the cangue, the two halves of which are folded together. Su-san's body is inclined slightly against the old man's left shoulder; her right foot points directly front, left foot is at an angle to it in the rear. With her left hand raised across the old warder's body, she carries out a graceful circular movement, the hand moving from left to right without actually making contact with the warder's body and moving to the rhythm of the music. A beatific smile gradually unfolds beneath the white make-up of the clown, ending in a burst of laughter as the old man finally relents and his anger vanishes beneath such devoted attention.*)

CH'UNG KUNG-TAO: Ho, ho, ho!
With the sweet words from her little mouth and her small hands caressing me, I can no longer feel annoyed. The world is full of

pleasure and my anger has vanished into the blue. If only it could last!

(*He is suddenly brought back to reality.*)

I say, Su-san, T'ai-yüan prefecture is not far away now, you'd better put on the cangue once more.

(*As Su-san straightens her pose there is a percussive passage ch'iao-t'ou pa, ta, k'ung, ch'iang, p'u, p'u, p'u, pa, ta, pa, ch'iang, ch'iang, ts'ai, ch'iang. The symbols are interpreted as follows: pa, ta is the consecutive beat of the right and left sticks on the drum; k'ung is the large and small gongs with the cymbals beaten lightly three times in unison; ch'iang is the two gongs and cymbals beaten forcefully in unison; p'u is the glancing contact of the cymbals; ts'ai is the combined beat of the small gong and cymbals.*)

SU-SAN: Father, father, ya!

CH'UNG KUNG-TAO: What is it?

SU-SAN (*speaking in the high-pitched, conventionalized manner of the tan roles*):

Because I was wrongly imprisoned without anyone to defend me, a friend in the jail wrote out a petition for me to redress my grievances before the T'ai-yüan magistrates. I have concealed it on my person as a precaution. In a little time I shall kneel before those important men. Father, please think of the best way for me to hand it to them.

CH'UNG KUNG-TAO: Let me see. Ah, I have an idea. Put the petition inside the cangue; then when you appear before the bench and are released from your chains the petition will drop out and you can hand it to the judges.

SU-SAN: Oh, thank you, father.

(*Ch'ung Kung-tao places the cangue on Su-san's shoulders once again and inserts the petition in the locking device. The hu-ch'in begins to play and Su-san sings in hsi-p'i yao-pan.*)

Just now a father and daughter reasoned together. Passersby listen in alarm. Far in the distance I can see T'ai-yüan city. Once arrived there, shall I live or die? Aiya!

(*A percussive passage accompanies her weeping, kua-erh, a rapid tattoo with both sticks on the drum, followed by her cry and concluding with tai, ch'iang, a beat on the small gong followed by the combined beat of gongs and cymbals.*

The two characters then exit up left, i.e., right of the audience, to a final percussive passage known as wei-sheng, literally "tail sound, or music," a name indicative enough of its function. It is a rhythmic sequence of brassy sound rendered onomatopoeically as follows: ta, tai, ch'iang, ts'ai, ch'iang, tai, tai, ts'ai, tai, i, tai, ch'iang, ts'ai, ch'iang i, ts'ai, ch'iang, ts'ai, ts'ai, ts'ai. Ta represents the drum beat, tai the small gong, ch'iang the large and small gong with the cymbals, and ts'ai the small gong with the cymbals; i signifies an extra strong reverberation.)

THE END

Index

COMPOSED BY HORNE ASSOCIATES, INC., HANOVER, NEW HAMPSHIRE
MANUFACTURED BY MALLOY LITHOGRAPHING, INC., ANN ARBOR, MICHIGAN
TEXT IS SET IN PRESS ROMAN, DISPLAY LINES IN PERPETUA

Library of Congress Cataloging in Publication Data (Revised)
Scott, Adolphe Clarence, 1909-   comp.
Traditional Chinese plays.
CONTENTS:—[1] Ssŭ lang visits his mother (Ssŭ lang
t'an mu). The butterfly dream (Hu tieh mêng).—
v. 2. Longing for worldly pleasures (Ssŭ fan). Fifteen
strings of cash (Shih wu kuan).—v. 3. Picking up
the jade bracelet (Shih yü-cho). A girl setting out
for trial (Nü ch'i-chieh).
1. Chinese drama—Translations into English.
2. English drama—Translations from Chinese.
I. Title.
PL2658.E5S34   895.1'2'052   66-22854
ISBN 0-299-06630-4 (vol. 3)